Thinking
& Eating

Thinking & Eating

The School of Life

Published in 2019 by The School of Life
70 Marchmont Street, London WC1N 1AB

Photography © Tristan Townley
Designed and typeset by Marcia Mihotich
Printed in Italy by Elcograf

A proportion of this book has appeared online at
www.theschooloflife.com/thebookoflife

The School of Life is a resource for helping us understand
ourselves, for improving our relationships, our careers and our
social lives – as well as for helping us find calm and get more
out of our leisure hours. We do this through creating films,
workshops, books and gifts.

www.theschooloflife.com

ISBN 978-1-912891-02-3

10 9 8 7 6 5 4 3 2 1

I

A

food

manifesto

1

This is an unusual book: it is both about food and comes from an organisation ordinarily devoted to psychology and philosophy.

At the School of Life, we are interested in how relationships work and how they go wrong; what the great thinkers of the past can teach us about how to live now; how our childhoods affect our present, and how we might address crises of loneliness, anxiety and despair. At first sight, these issues don't seem to have much to do with recipes and suggestions of what might be nice for dinner. But, as we will seek to explain, they very much do.

2

Intellectuals have rarely engaged with food, because our culture has long kept the aspirations of the mind at a distance from the satisfactions of the body. It has seemed as if one cannot be both a cook and a thinker.

Consider two contrasting attitudes to the spaces in which food, on the one hand, and ideas, on the other, are presented to us. A restaurant committed to charming the palate will typically give a lot of attention to decor. Effort will go into starching the napkins; someone will think about how the waiters should be dressed and what kind of music will play in the background. At the same time, it would feel odd if the management were to show concern about the intellectual or psychological life of its customers; if the waiter, for example, offered a lecture on 'the problems of self-knowledge' before taking orders or, if instead of asking 'how is your meal?', a standard question were 'how is your soul?'

By contrast, a modern university lecture hall – the prime location for the expansion of our minds – is generally functional in design.

The implied idea is that it doesn't really matter what the room looks like so long as the students can hear what's being said and the display

A modern restaurant and lecture hall: the divorce of the sensory from the intellectual.

screen is visible. Whether the place is beautiful or ugly is felt to be incidental to the task at hand: the transmission of ideas. It would seem strange if the head of department were to focus on ambient lighting or had strict rules about the colour coordination of the lecturers' clothes; we'd not expect there to be long meetings on whether the texture of the walls really suited a course on Existentialism or a survey of the ideas of Melanie Klein.

3

A stark division between the intellect and the senses hasn't always been in place. During the Renaissance, the government of the city of Florence, under intense pressure from the larger states that surrounded it, grew interested in promoting a deeper loyalty to the idea of freedom among its population. They wanted to persuade their citizens to adopt a more ambitious and resolute attitude to Florence's political position and to honour their own distinctive way of life. But when the government of Florence made its argument public, it did not produce a learned intellectual treatise. It commissioned the city's greatest artist, Michelangelo, to make a statue of a young hero from a biblical story with which everyone at the time would have been familiar: David, the young boy devoted to his own independence, who single-handedly defied the superpower of his time.

When the statue was placed in front of government buildings in 1504, it was the most erotically charged and alluring work of art in Europe. It also managed to sum up a complex political programme in the blink of an eye, magisterially conveying ideas via a flow of marble rather than words.

4

The notion of using the sensuous realm to articulate an intellectual point had been developed in Florence a few years earlier by the most famous philosopher of the era, Marsilio Ficino (perhaps significantly, Ficino is not well known today). Ficino held that 'we rise to ideas by means of the senses'; that is, ideas take root in our minds when our sensuous and emotional instincts have been adroitly stimulated. We are not inherently or only logical beings. We are emotional creatures who need to be charmed into accepting concepts. Without sensuous support, ideas – however worthy – will be largely ineffective. Intellectuals, whatever their initial

Michelangelo, *David*, 1501–4.

inhibitions, need to recognise the power of art, music, architecture and – somewhere along the way – of lunch and dinner.

5
Ficino's concept of the importance of sensuality was still powerful a couple of hundred years later. In the 18th century, the Catholic Church in Bavaria grew more ambitious about transforming the inner lives of its constituents. It wished to increase people's commitment to forgiving their neighbours, to examining their consciences, and to adopting a humble attitude towards their failings – all important but not naturally appealing moves. However, the church leaders did not simply produce stern sermons or academic essays; they built the delightful building we know today as the Church of the Fourteen Saints.

They understood that we are best moved to compassion when we are touched by beauty, not when we are given a text to read. They ensured that their building would be as elegant, sweet and charming as possible because they believed that our readiness to accept ideas depends on the state of mind generated by our senses. The play of light, the feeling of grandeur, the pleasure of being in an airy space all serve a higher purpose: they

Balthasar Neumann, Church of the Fourteen Saints, Bavaria, 1743–72.

put us in the mood for uplifting but demanding ideas.

We are a long way here from the attitude underpinning the design of the modern university lecture theatre.

6
At the School of Life, we have been guided by the examples of Michelangelo, Ficino and the Bavarian church – and we have grown interested in how the sensory realm can be deployed to help with the transmission of ideas. That's how we started thinking about, among other dishes, fish pie and miso soup.

7
Typically, however much we enjoy eating, we don't normally think that what we put on our plates is particularly meaningful. One person who took a different view was the 19th-

century German philosopher Friedrich Nietzsche. In January 1877, while he was staying in Italy, Nietzsche (then in his early thirties) wrote a letter to his mother mentioning that he had discovered something he considered central to human happiness. Had Nietzsche stumbled on his legendary notion that modern life is driven by envy and resentment? Or that God has died? Or that we must aspire to being Supermen? In fact, his discovery was to do with cooking: he had been learning how to make the perfect risotto.

For Nietzsche, risotto encapsulated an attitude to life. When properly prepared, it is richly savoury yet light; delicate yet satisfying; it leaves us feeling clean and energetic. The qualities of the dish were an invitation to become a certain kind of person: less ponderous, more direct, lively and playful. Nietzsche wanted his writing and his personality to be like risotto. It occurred to him that the prose of his academic colleagues back in Germany was more like over-cooked vegetables or heavy servings of boiled meat – and that was why German philosophy had failed. The massive, impenetrable tomes of Hegel or Kant struck him as being like the worst kinds of meals; the kind that leave us stuffed, listless and gloomy and in need of a lie-down in a darkened room.

Nietzsche's realisation was that material matters are the bearers of ideas about life, and that the material things we habitually consume will therefore influence our intellectual outlook – for better or worse.

8
Nietzsche was making a crucial adjustment to the standard intellectual critique of 'materialism'. Typically, those who are ambitious around ideas take issue with our love of objects and the desire to have enough money to pay for and enjoy them. But Nietzsche's point is that – sometimes, at least – it is to material things that we need to turn for help with the development of our souls. He wanted us to see an important possibility: that of a 'good' kind of materialism.

9
Materialism goes well when the physical, bodily, sensuous things we are attracted to (and want to buy, own and consume) are themselves the containers of and ambassadors for the psychological ideas we need. That is what is meant by good materialism.

10
Sometimes we meet good materialism in art.

The Danish artist Købke painted his *View of Østerbro from Dosseringen*

Christen Købke, *View of Østerbro from Dosseringen*, 1838.

in 1838. It shows a group of people standing on a jetty doing something with a small boat. Beyond that, it takes an implicit philosophy of life – marked by patience, modesty and contentment with the everyday – and allows us to absorb its spirit through our eyes. If we were to pin the postcard of the picture somewhere in the hall and catch sight of it regularly on our way out, a precious mood would stand a chance of more reliably becoming our own.

This noble kind of materialism isn't restricted to the fine arts. An item of clothing might be just as powerful in its capacity to materialise an attitude and embed it in our lives.

In the 1960s, the English designer Mary Quant sought to express a range of ideas about how to live.

She sought to promote a classless attitude that was unfussy yet elegant, confident yet attuned to vulnerability and desire. Her clothes alluded to an ideology via the language of colours, textures and hemlines. By buying one of her dresses, one wasn't merely following fashion, one was testifying in a small but real way to a wish to become a new person.

Likewise, a decorative object at home needn't merely be a status symbol or a trophy. It can embody ideas and emotions that we feel we need more of in our lives. A small celadon bowl, for example, is the material carrier of a calm, poised state of mind. It invites us to be a little more like it. It doesn't

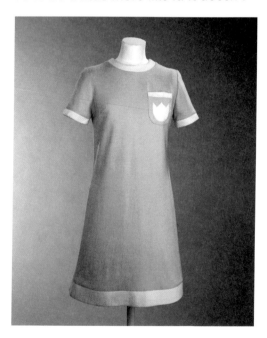

Mary Quant, mini-dress, 1966.

try to argue us into calming down or tell us to stop fidgeting; it just quietly invites us to be more like it appears: poised, balanced and restful.

Celadon bowl.

11
Significantly, the ideas we encounter via a dress, a bowl or – like Nietzsche – a risotto, are not necessarily complex or intellectually difficult. In fact, they are often things that we theoretically know already. They are structurally simple commitments about kindness, calm, courage or openness to experience.

That they should be simultaneously so obvious and yet so often forgotten is one of the grim ironies of the human condition. There are a host of ideas that we already consent to in principle: that we should forgive rather than extract revenge, or that we should listen to others rather than assert our egos. However, in practice, we continually forget such vital

truths. Our minds are like colanders: our better thoughts drain away quickly and our lives suffer as a consequence.

12
The purpose of culture is to keep on returning us – as often as possible – to our own best convictions: to keep them at the front of our minds so they can work an effect on our distracted and corrupt characters.

13
This is why the School of Life embarked on a cookbook: we are interested in the way in which what we eat and what we cook interacts with our psychological needs. A dish can serve the same kind of purpose as a work of art, an item of clothing or a building: it too can 'materialise' – and hence render more permanent – an outlook we need in order to flourish.

14
In recent times, our society has been eager to recruit food to the project of physical health. However, by comparison, we have not paid much attention to how cooking and eating can assist us with the project of emotional intelligence and psychological well-being.

We want to show how ingredients and dishes can be supporters of certain ideas, emotions and states of mind that help us confront the challenges of existence. We're committed to the ways in which food can store, memorialise and transmit the most important ideas of our lives.

II

Recipes

We know that certain foods can be good for us. But when using the word 'good', we often define things in too limited a way. Typically, we focus on the physical benefits of nutrition: we welcome particular ingredients that are low in calories or high in fibre, that can provide a useful dose of potassium or decrease the risk of angina.

There is a larger possibility to be explored around the concept of goodness: *that food may have a role to play in helping us to become better people.*

What does being a better person involve? One answer is that it means possessing a range of good qualities of mind – or what the Ancient Greek philosopher Aristotle legendarily termed 'virtues'. In his *Nicomachean Ethics*, Aristotle identified twelve virtues that he saw as defining the ideal good citizen of his time:

Ingredients of the 'Good Person'
(Aristotle, Ancient Greece)

Courage	Good temper
Temperance	Truthfulness
Liberality	Wit
Magnificence	Friendliness
Magnanimity	Modesty
Proper ambition	Righteous indignation

Unsurprisingly, given how much life has changed, Aristotle's list doesn't quite capture the virtues that would most help us now. A modern list of virtues might look more like this:

Ingredients of the 'Good Person'
(The Modern World)

Hope	Kindness
Playfulness	Patience
Maturity	Pessimism
Reassurance	Self-knowledge
Diplomacy	Self-love
Cynicism	Assertiveness
Sensitivity	Compassion
Intelligence	Appreciation

A key point that Aristotle made remains true today: we tend to forget to practise the virtues that we are, in theory, committed to. In principle, we want to be better people and to grow emotionally. However, the idea of self-improvement quickly slips from our minds amid the bustle and tensions of existence. That's why Aristotle believed that we need help not only in learning what the virtues are, but also in fixing them in our fickle minds. That's why he recommended that a good society should not only have a standard education system, it should also make use of the more subtly pedagogic qualities of music, festivals, plays, dance, artworks and oratory – all of which he believed could bolster the case for qualities we already admire but don't regularly remember to act upon.

Like music or painting, food can suggest a range of ideas about life in the broadest sense – ideas of which we are reminded in a visceral way every time we connect with them through our palates.

Religions have always understood this, which is why they have so often incorporated foods into rituals that aim to reform and improve our characters. Zen Buddhism, for example, wishes to turn us into calm and communally minded people. It doesn't merely try to inspire these virtues in us through lectures and books; it also asks its adherents to grow more serene and kind by brewing and drinking tea together. The ritual drinking of green tea is one of Zen's central ceremonies – as important to the creed as a mass might be for Catholics. The way one is meant to prepare the tea – unhurriedly waiting for the water to boil, readying the cups, gently stirring the crushed leaves – is intended to provide a lesson in patience and gentle togetherness. The cups and utensils are recommended to be deliberately humble, so as to turn the mind towards simplicity, while in the silent drinking of the tea, those who are present are encouraged to concentrate on the moment, to still their day-to-day thoughts and to become aware of each other's consoling presence and affectionate natures. Around a fairly ordinary beverage, Zen had the monumental idea of creating a ritual to anchor us more firmly to some central human virtues.

The Zen tea ceremony: a reminder of calm and friendship delivered via green tea.

Judaism has acted likewise. It has wanted to remind its people of God's covenant to the tribes of Israel, and of the need to remain faithful to a Talmudic vision of goodness. But this doctrinal point isn't merely emphasised through words. Food is also invited to play a crucial educative role. During the Passover meal, tradition mandates (among a host of other details) that participants give a pride of place to horseradish, whose bitter taste is meant to symbolise the harshness of the Jews' captivity in Egypt. By remembering this suffering while spooning horseradish onto a piece of unleavened bread, we are prompted towards greater sympathy with the sorrows of one's ancestors and of humanity more broadly. Horseradish is invited to lend support to the virtue of compassion.

Although religions have been ambitious about building connections between foods and ideas, and in their use of particular recipes to underpin a philosophy of life, the moves they have made are not limited to their own tenets and doctrines. Even outside of theology, we can link certain virtues with foods and co-opt the business of eating with the project of self-improvement and the development of inner virtue.

Considered with imagination, some ingredients appear to convey virtues we might want to remind ourselves of regularly. These ingredients stand as symbols of ideas that sustain our characters. In using them in our cooking, we're addressing our bodies but also inspiring our spirit; we are delighting our senses while inviting a shift in our psyches.

There are sixteen ingredients to which the School of Life is especially drawn in its cooking; they seem to evoke sixteen virtues that feel as if they deserve a more secure place in our lives. What follows is a list of ingredients, a discussion of the virtues they seem to symbolise, and a selection of recipes that may be able to promote them.

1
The key ingredients

The Lemon
Symbol of Hope

We're often schooled to be sceptical about the virtue of hope. It can seem naive and childlike to be hopeful. Such worries seem misplaced, however. Too many of our plans get derailed not because they are unworkable or misguided but because our reserves of hope have been depleted. We can't keep faith with the arduousness of our lives and its projects and give up before we can do ourselves justice.

The lemon is an ultimate symbol of hope, and on this basis deserves a place in our kitchens and our endeavours. It carries with it the sense of having ripened slowly in the sunshine; as if it had absorbed and condensed the warmest and most confident days of summer. These it appears to have artfully compressed, doing in the realm of taste what a camera does with time. Even on the saddest, most fog-bound winter days, a lemon on the window ledge speaks of moments when we still dared to have faith in ourselves, and bids us to recover a connection to our former positivity.

With its brilliant outer colour and its forceful bracing inner joy, the lemon is our ally in the continuing struggle against giving up. We'll get through this; it will eventually be the weekend; disagreements worse than this can get resolved. The lemon is a friend in our mind's attempts to structure arguments why it might, after all, be worth enduring. Maybe the anxiety will end. Perhaps the project will work out. The arguments might stop. Our enemies could get bored and turn elsewhere. Our reputation might recover. The mood could lift. A lot of things could, in the end, be more or less OK – bearable, even. All this the lemon knows how to whisper.

Recipes
Preserved lemon pasta 26
Lemon curd 27
Lemon drizzle cake 28

Preserved lemon pasta

Ingredients:

350 g | 12 oz spaghetti, or linguine
4 tbsp olive oil
3 cloves garlic, minced
1 tbsp anchovy fillets, in oil, drained
and finely chopped (optional)
½ preserved lemon, finely chopped
4 tbsp Parmesan, grated, plus extra
to serve
1 handful flat-leaf parsley, chopped

salt
freshly ground black pepper

Prep time: 10 minutes
Cook time: 10 minutes
Makes: 4 servings

1   Cook the spaghetti in a large saucepan of salted, boiling water until just tender to the bite (*al dente*), about 10 minutes.

2   Drain well and reserve a small cup of the starchy cooking water.

3   Heat the olive oil in a large high-sided frying or sauté pan set over a medium heat until hot.

4   Add the garlic and anchovy, if using, cooking and stirring for 30 seconds. Stir in the preserved lemon and continue cook for a further 30 seconds until fragrant.

5   Add the drained spaghetti and a most of the reserved cooking water, stirring and shaking the pan over a medium heat until glossy in appearance, about 2 minutes.

6   Remove from the heat and sprinkle over the Parmesan, stirring well to create a creamy sauce; if needed, add more of the reserved cooking water to loosen.

7   When ready to serve, season to taste with salt and pepper. Divide between bowls and top with parsley and more Parmesan.

Lemon curd

Ingredients:
100 g | ½ cup butter
350 g | 1 ½ cups sugar
2 tsp lemon zest
7 unwaxed lemons, juiced
4 very fresh eggs
40 ml Cointreau (optional)

Prep time: 10 minutes
Cook time: 15 minutes
Makes: 3 × 350 g jars

1   Melt the butter in a bain-marie along with the sugar, lemon zest and the lemon juice.

2   Beat the eggs and add them gradually to the mixture until it takes on a creamy consistency. Stir in the Cointreau at this point if you're using.

3   Pour the mixture into sterilised jars, close tightly and store in a cool, dark place.

Tips
To sterilise jars, wash them in hot, soapy water or put through the hot cycle of a dishwasher. Do not dry off – instead, place the wet jars into an oven set to 160°C (140° fan) | 325F | gas 3 for 15 minutes. Leave to cool before filling.

Lemon drizzle cake

Ingredients:

For the cake:

240 g | 1 cup unsalted butter, softened, plus 1 tbsp extra

240 g | 1 ½ cups self-raising flour, plus 2 tbsp extra

240 g | 1 cup caster sugar

½ tsp baking powder

1 pinch salt

4 large eggs

2 tbsp whole milk

1 lemon, zest, finely grated

For the drizzle:

4 small lemons, juiced

180 g | ¾ cup caster sugar

Prep time: 10 minutes

Cook time: 55 minutes

Makes: 12 servings

1   For the cake: Preheat the oven to 180°C (160° fan) | 350F | gas 4. Grease and line the base of a 23 cm | 9" round, deep, springform cake tin with greaseproof paper.

2   Grease the sides of the tin with 1 tablespoon softened butter. Dust with 2 tablespoons flour, tilting and turning the tin to coat all sides evenly; tip out any excess flour.

3   Combine the butter, flour, sugar, baking powder, salt, eggs, milk and lemon zest in a large mixing bowl. Stir well to combine before beating on high with an electric whisk until smooth and creamy, about 3–4 minutes.

4   Spoon into the prepared tin and tap the tin on a work surface a few times to help settle the batter.

5   Bake for about 45–55 minutes until risen and dry to the touch on top; a cake tester should come out clean from its centre. Remove to a wire rack to cool.

6   For the drizzle: As the cake cools, mix the lemon juice and sugar in a bowl, stirring briefly to combine.

7   Poke holes all over the surface of the cake with a cake tester. Pour the drizzle mixture all over the cake, leaving it to seep down into the cake.

8   Once the cake is cool, turn it out from its tin onto a cake stand and slice before serving.

The Lime
Symbol of Playfulness

The lime is less famous than its sibling, the lemon; it feels younger, less responsible, but also more playful.

Lemon goes well with many things; around the lime, on the other hand, we can make mistakes. Lime can be unexpectedly delightful in a salad dressing, but disappointing when squeezed on grilled fish. A slice of lime in a cool drink is more sophisticated than a wedge of lemon, but it's almost impossible to make a successful lime tart. However, paired with the right companions, a lime transforms the mood in the direction of jest and good humour. We may realise how easily and unfairly we forget about limes.

Playfulness – like the lime – doesn't often come to the front of our minds. We may associate play too exclusively with childhood, underestimating its contribution to adult life. Playfulness involves taking risks with another's dignity and our own. We dare to make a provocative comment; we reveal a vulnerable part of our character to someone we don't know well; we try humour around a sober-looking person. We haven't played it safe, but we can be rewarded with those sudden moments of sincerity and closeness that are the gifts of well-angled playfulness.

The lime encourages loyalty to an unheralded but central part of our nature.

Recipes:
Nam pla prik 32
Pico de gallo 33
Key lime pie 34

Nam pla prik
(Thai dipping sauce)

Ingredients:

4 tbsp lime juice

2 tbsp fish sauce

2 ½ tsp soft brown sugar, or palm sugar if available

1 tbsp warm water

5 cloves garlic, minced

2–3 Thai bird's eye chillies, seeded and thinly sliced

1 small handful coriander, chopped

Prep time: 5 minutes

Makes: 2 servings

1   Stir together lime juice, fish sauce, sugar and warm water in a small serving bowl until the sugar dissolves.

2   Stir in the garlic, chillies and coriander. Serve fresh for best results.

Tips

The quantities can be doubled or tripled for larger batches. Adjust the amount of chilli to suit your tastes. This dipping sauce is an ideal accompaniment to all sorts of Thai dishes – from spring rolls to noodles.

Pico de gallo
(Mexican salsa)

Ingredients:

3 medium vine tomatoes
½ medium white onion, diced
1 jalapeño, seeded and finely diced
2 tbsp lime juice
1 pinch caster sugar
1 handful coriander, chopped
1 tsp white vinegar
sea salt

Prep time: 10 minutes
Chill time: 1 hour
Makes: 4 servings

1   Stir everything together, apart from the salt, in a serving bowl until thoroughly combined. Season to taste.

2   For best results, cover and chill for at least 1 hour before serving.

Tips

A vibrant salsa that is perfect spooned over tacos (p188–189), scrambled eggs or fried potatoes.

Key lime pie

Ingredients:

For the base:

250 g | 1 ½ cups digestive biscuits, crushed

80 g | ⅓ cup unsalted butter, melted

2 tbsp soft brown sugar

For the curd filling:

3 gelatine leaves

250 ml | 1 cup fresh lime juice, about 8–10 limes

60 g | ½ cup cornflour

200 g | 1 cup caster sugar

180 g | ¾ cup unsalted butter, cubed

6 medium egg yolks

3 medium eggs

250 g | 1 cup cream cheese, softened

Prep time: 40 minutes

Chill time: 8 hours

Makes: 1 pie, approx. 12 servings

1   For the base: Combine the biscuits, melted butter and soft brown sugar in a food processor. Pulse several times until the mixture resembles rough breadcrumbs.

2   Pack the mixture into the base of a 20 cm | 8" springform cake tin using the back of a damp tablespoon. Chill until needed.

3   For the curd filling: Soak the gelatine leaves in a small bowl of water.

4   Combine the lime juice, cornflour and caster sugar in a heavy-based saucepan.

5   Add 100 ml | 7 tbsp water and bring to a simmer over a moderate heat, whisking continuously until you have a thickened sauce.

6   Once the mixture starts to bubble, remove from the heat and beat in the butter, cube by cube, until smooth and glossy.

7   Whisk together the egg yolks and eggs in a separate mixing bowl. Gradually whisk into the lime mixture and return the pan to the heat.

8   Continue to whisk until the curd thickens and falls from the whisk when tapped against the side of the saucepan.

9   Remove from the heat. Remove the gelatine from the water, squeeze out the excess water, and whisk into the curd until dissolved. Let the mixture cool for 10 minutes before beating in the cream cheese.

10 Spoon the curd on top of the biscuit base. Rap the tin a few times to help settle the filing. Cover and chill overnight.

11 To serve: When ready to serve, turn out the pie and top with lime zest before slicing.

The Fig
Symbol of Maturity

The fig is a symbol of maturity. A tree might reach its maximum height in 80 years. Its fruit is gentle, unassuming and recessive in nature – and yet, once one becomes attuned to its quiet delicacy, it can be prized as the most accomplished of fruits.

Much of what maturity is concerned with is embodied in the fig. The fruit's outer skin is modest and unshowy, giving few hints of the brighter, richer, sweeter interior. This is an ingredient that requires that people drop their normal agitation and clamour in order to hear the goodness it has to impart. The fig is sweet – but only gently, like a quiet smile or an understanding look rather than a broad grin or a shout of joy. The fig holds back; it is in no hurry and has no need to thrust itself on our attention.

Mature people are less interested in claiming the attention of others; they listen more and speak less. They aren't prone to ecstasy or effusion. Without being miserable, they are aware of the tendencies of plans to go wrong, of hopes to fade, and of seemingly great ideas to lead to very little. Partly for that reason, the mature are invested in kindness and gentleness. They are experts at reassurance and containment.

In an ideal secular religion, the fig would be a central symbol; we would strive to become as it already is.

Recipes:

Roast duck with fig, port and star anise 38
Fig and almond tart 40

Roast duck with fig, port and star anise

Ingredients:

1 whole duck, jointed, carcass
reserved for another recipe, see Tips
2 tbsp sunflower oil
200 ml | ⅞ cup tawny port
1 large orange, juiced
4 whole star anise
4 fresh figs, quartered
thyme sprigs, to garnish
sea salt
freshly ground black pepper

Prep time: 30 minutes
Cook time: 1 hour 15 minutes
Makes: 4 servings

1   Preheat the oven to 190°C (170° fan) | 375F | gas 5.

2   Rub the duck pieces with sunflower oil and season them generously with salt and pepper.

3   Preheat an ovenproof cast-iron pan over a moderate heat until hot. Sear the duck pieces in the pan until golden-brown all over, turning occasionally with tongs.

4   Remove from the pan to a plate. Deglaze the pan with the port, letting it bubble and reduce by half. Stir in the orange juice, star anise and figs.

5   Arrange the duck legs on top of the figs and transfer the pan to the oven. Roast for 1 hour; in the meantime, wrap the duck breasts with aluminium foil to keep warm.

6   After 1 hour, arrange the duck breasts in the pan and return the pan to the oven for a further 12–15 minutes until the duck breasts are firm to the touch with a slight spring when pressed.

7   Remove the pan from the oven and let the duck pieces rest for at least 10 minutes before slicing the breasts and serving alongside the legs, pan juices, figs and and a garnish of thyme.

Tips
If needed, you can ask your butcher to joint your duck for you. You can also buy the legs and breasts separately if a whole duck isn't available.

Fig and almond tart

Ingredients:

For the pastry:

225 g | 8 oz | 1 ⅔ cups plain flour, plus extra for dusting

120 g | 4 oz | ½ cup unsalted butter, cold and cubed

2 tbsp caster sugar

¼ tsp salt

1 large egg

1–2 tbsp iced water, as needed

For the fig filling:

150 ml | 5 fl oz | ⅔ cup double cream

150 g | 5 oz | ½ cup honey

6 gelatine leaves, soaked in cold water for 10 minutes

8 fresh figs

475 g | 17 oz | 2 cups Greek yoghurt

240 g | 8 oz | 1 cup mascarpone

1 pinch salt

½ tsp almond extract

To decorate:

4 fresh figs, sliced

80 g | 3 oz | ½ cup flaked almonds, lightly toasted

Prep time: 30 minutes

Cook time: 30 minutes

Chill time: 4 hours 30 minutes

Makes: 1 tart, approx. 12 servings

1   For the pastry: Combine the flour, butter, sugar and salt in a food processor. Pulse until the mixture resembles rough breadcrumbs.

2   Add the egg and pulse until a rough dough starts to form around the blade of the processor. Add a little iced water and pulse again to bring it together; it should be soft but not sticky.

3   Turn out the dough from the processor and shape it into a disc. Wrap in clingfilm and chill for 30 minutes.

4   After chilling, preheat the oven to 180°C (160° fan) | 350F | gas 4.

5   Turn out the dough onto a lightly floured surface and roll out into a ½ cm | ¼" thick round. Use it to line the base and sides of a 20 cm | 8" springform tart tin.

6   Cut away any excess, overhanging pastry and prick the base all over with a fork. Line with greaseproof paper and fill with baking beans.

7   Blind bake for about 15 minutes until golden at the edges. Remove from the oven and discard the paper and beans.

8   Return to the oven to brown the base, 3–5 minutes. Remove to a wire rack to cool.

9   For the fig filling: Warm the cream and honey in a small saucepan set over a medium heat, stirring occasionally. Once simmering, remove from the heat and add the soaked gelatine leaves, whisking until fully dissolved.

10 Split the figs in half and scoop out their flesh into a food processor. Add the cream mixture and remaining ingredients for the filling.

11 Cover and process on high until smooth, scraping down the sides of the processor as needed.

12 Turn out the filling into the pastry, smoothing it flat with the back of a damp tablespoon or an offset spatula. Cover and chill for 4 hours.

13 To decorate: When ready to serve, turn out the tart and decorate with fig slices and flaked almonds.

The Avocado
Symbol of Reassurance

The opposite of panic is not the belief that everything will be fine; it is the calm assessment of the challenges of a situation accompanied by a sense that we have the resources to cope with whatever comes our way. Too often, agitation itself becomes the obstacle to our survival. But if we can find the means to soothe ourselves, we can reassure others and then step out of the vicious pattern of escalation, where one person's distress feeds and develops another's.

A capacity for reassurance is the fruit of a proper sense that we are now adults, and have the strength, freedom and intelligence to plot a way through our difficulties. Avocados are apt symbols of the reassuring manoeuvres of the mind. Their flesh is firm, steady and, at points, yielding. Their taste is mild, the texture creamy and their effect profoundly nourishing. A hunger that was gnawing at us wildly only a few minutes before is expertly assuaged by its calmly authoritative presence.

Avocados are what we should turn to – and remember to be a little more like – in the midst of our frequent and bewildering crises.

Recipes:

Avocado pasta 44
Crab and avocado salad 45

Avocado pasta

Ingredients:
450 g | 16 oz | 6 cups fusilli
2 ripe avocados
75 ml | 2 ½ fl oz | ⅓ cup extra-virgin olive oil
50 g | 1 ¾ oz | ½ cup Parmesan, grated, plus extra to serve
1 large clove garlic, minced
1 large handful basil leaves
½ lemon, juiced
salt
freshly ground black pepper

Cook time: 10 minutes
Prep time: 10 minutes
Makes: 4 servings

1   Cook the pasta in a large saucepan of salted, boiling water until tender to the bite (*al dente*), about 10–12 minutes.

2   In the meantime, halve, pit, peel and dice the avocados. Combine the flesh with the olive oil, Parmesan, garlic, basil, lemon juice and some salt and pepper to taste in a food processor.

3   Cover and blend on high until thick and creamy. Adjust the seasoning to taste with more salt and pepper as needed. Turn out into a mixing bowl.

4   Drain the pasta when ready and transfer to the avocado purée, thoroughly stirring until combined.

5   Divide between bowls and serve with more grated Parmesan, if desired.

Crab and avocado salad

Ingredients:

2 tbsp mayonnaise
2 tbsp buttermilk
1 tbsp crème fraîche
1 tbsp lemon juice
½ tsp Dijon mustard
1 dash Worcestershire sauce
225 g | 8 oz | 1 ½ cups white crab meat, picked over to remove shell and cartilage
2 celery stalks, finely diced
4 chives, snipped

1 large ripe avocado
2 little gem lettuce, leaves separated
extra-virgin olive oil, for drizzling
salt
freshly ground black pepper

Prep time: 10 minutes
Cook time: 10 minutes
Makes: 4 servings

1   Whisk together the mayonnaise, buttermilk, crème fraîche, lemon juice, mustard, Worcestershire sauce and a generous pinch of salt and pepper to taste in a large mixing bowl.

2   Add the crab meat, celery and chives to the dressing, gently folding with a spatula to combine. Halve, pit, peel and dice the avocado flesh. Add to the bowl, folding to combine.

3   Line small serving plates with lettuce leaves. Spoon the crab salad on top and drizzle with extra-virgin olive oil before serving.

Olive oil
Symbol of Diplomacy

The olive has a flavour, identity and charm of its own. As an oil, it most often serves to enhance and develop the merits of other foods: it makes the bland lettuce leaf more enticing; it turns a dry slice of bread sweet and dough-like; in a pan, olive oil transforms the bitter, pale onion into something sugary and golden; it turns a slice of humble potato into an alluring crisp; it protects the bottom of a frying pan and stops the salmon's skin separating from its flank. Olive oil allows divergent ingredients to get on well together: under its influence, even the tomato and red pepper will stop quarrelling and learn to cooperate.

In the olive, and its natural oil, we can see the edible equivalent of the human virtue of diplomacy. We might associate diplomacy with ambassadors and international relationships, but really it is a virtue that belongs in everyday life. Diplomacy means bringing out the less obvious potential of other people, reducing unnecessary friction and harmonising potentially opposing points of view.

Olive oil brings the virtue of diplomacy closer to the front of our unhelpfully abrasive minds.

Recipes
Focaccia 48
Patatas a lo pobre (poor man's potatoes) 49
Olive oil cake 50

Focaccia

Ingredients:

450 g | 3 cups white bread flour, plus extra for dusting

2 tsp salt

2 ½ tsp dried active yeast

250 ml | 1 cup warm water

4 tbsp extra-virgin olive oil

1 large handful rosemary sprigs

Prep and cook time: 30 minutes

Proving time: 1 hour

Makes: 1 large loaf

1   Combine the flour and salt in a large mixing bowl. Combine the yeast with 60 ml | ¼ cup of the warm water and 3 tablespoons of the extra-virgin olive oil in a measuring jug. Leave for 10 minutes in a warm place until frothy. Make a well in the flour and add the yeasty water to it along with the remaining warm water, mixing well until a dough comes together.

2   Turn out onto a lightly floured surface and knead for 8–10 minutes until you have a soft, smooth dough.

3   Place the dough in a clean bowl and leave to prove in a warm place, loosely covered with clingfilm, until doubled in size, about 1 hour.

4   Preheat the oven to 200°C (180° fan) | 400F | gas 6.

5   Turn out the dough after proving and knock back. Shape into a round and place in a 23 cm | 9" baking dish that has been brushed with a little of the remaining oil. Make indents all over the top of the dough using your knuckle.

6   Brush over the last of the oil and stud the indents with the rosemary sprigs before baking for around 25–30 minutes, or until golden.

Patatas a lo pobre
(poor man's potatoes)

Ingredients:

250 ml | 9 fl oz | 1 cup extra-virgin
olive oil
450 g | 16 oz | 3 cups waxy potatoes,
e.g. New Potatoes, cut into ¼ cm | ⅛"
thick slices
1 large onion, sliced
1 large green pepper, cored, seeded
and sliced
3 cloves garlic, crushed

sea salt
freshly ground black pepper

Prep time: 10 minutes
Cook time: 20 minutes
Makes: 4 servings

1   Heat the oil in a large high-sided frying or sauté pan set over a medium
heat until hot. Add the potatoes, onion, green pepper and garlic.

2   Cook at a steady simmer until the potatoes are tender to the tip of a knife,
about 15–20 minutes.

3   Using a slotted spoon, divide the potatoes, onion and green pepper
between plates. Season with salt and pepper before serving.

Olive oil cake

Ingredients:

325 ml | 11 fl oz | 1 ⅓ cups extra-virgin olive oil, plus extra for greasing
240 g | 8 oz | 1 cup caster sugar, plus 2 tbsp extra for the tin
275 g | 10 oz | 2 cups cake flour, or plain flour
40 g | 1 ½ oz | ⅓ cup ground almonds
2 tsp baking powder
½ tsp bicarbonate of soda
½ tsp sea salt
3 tbsp sweet vermouth, or amaretto
3 tbsp crème fraîche
2 tsp vanilla extract
3 large eggs
icing sugar, to serve

Prep time: 20 minutes
Cook time: 50 minutes
Makes: 1 cake, approx. 12 servings

1   Preheat the oven to 190°C (170° fan) | 375F | gas 5. Grease and line the base of a 23 cm | 9" springform cake tin with greaseproof paper.

2   Grease the base and sides of the tin with olive oil and sprinkle with 2 tablespoons sugar, tilting and rotating the tin to coat with the sugar; discard the excess.

3   Whisk together the cake flour, ground almonds, baking powder, bicarbonate of soda and salt in a large mixing bowl.

4   Stir together the vermouth, crème fraîche and vanilla extract in a small bowl. Set aside until needed.

5   Combine the eggs and sugar in a large mixing bowl. Beat together with an electric mixer until pale, thick and leaving ribbons in the trail of the beaters, about 3–5 minutes.

6   Gradually beat in the olive oil in a slow, steady stream until fully incorporated. On a low speed, beat in the flour mixture in three additions, alternating with the vermouth mixture, until a mostly smooth batter forms. Spoon the batter into the prepared tin.

7   Bake until firm and golden on top, and a toothpick comes out clean from the centre, about 40–50 minutes.

8   Remove from the oven and let cool in the tin, set on a wire rack, before turning out and serving. If desired, lightly dust with icing sugar before slicing.

The Caper
Symbol of Cynicism

The caper offers us a precise model, in edible form, of how certain virtues function. Cynicism on its own is not a recipe for being a better person; the purely cynical person is a disaster. Through their eyes, everyone is egotistical and everything that looks decent or benign is just a hypocritical mask. But if we have no cynical instincts at all, we're liable to be shocked by the normal imperfections of others and of society, and our naivety will prevent us from mounting necessary interventions and protests.

What we're looking for is a touch of cynicism: a capacity for an accurate, unfrightened recognition that there is a dark and self-interested aspect to human nature. The partial cynic understands that all institutions have drawbacks and flaws, even though they have merits as well; they take it for granted that people's motives are not always pure; they realise that the search for personal gain is often present in acts of charity, though altruism is there as well.

A whole dish of capers will be hard to swallow, but used sparingly they create intriguing contrasts. Cured in vinegar, they add a vitally sour accent to what might otherwise be passive, bland dishes. They banish unwarranted innocence and tedium; they can make us wince and smile in a clear-eyed way.

Recipes:
White fish with lemon, caper and butter sauce 54
Octopus with caper berries, paprika and parsley 55
Baked feta cheese with sun-dried tomato and capers 56
Salsa verde 57

White fish with lemon, caper and butter sauce

Ingredients:

4 skinless white fish fillets, e.g. cod or haddock, pin-boned

4 tbsp olive oil, divided

4 tbsp butter

2 tbsp baby capers, drained and rinsed

4 tbsp lemon juice

1 tsp lemon zest, finely grated

1 tbsp fresh tarragon, finely chopped (optional)

sea salt

freshly ground black pepper

Prep time: 10 minutes

Cook time: 15 minutes

Makes: 4 servings

1   Preheat the oven to 200°C (180° fan) | 400F | gas 6.

2   Rub the fish fillets with 2 tablespoons olive oil and place in a cast-iron pan or small baking dish. Season with salt and pepper.

3   Bake until firm to the touch, opaque in appearance and starting to flake, about 12–15 minutes.

4   In the meantime, melt the butter with the remaining olive oil in a small saucepan set over a medium heat.

5   Add the capers and cook for 1 minute, stirring from time to time. Remove from the heat and gently stir in the lemon juice, lemon zest, tarragon (if using), and some salt and pepper to taste. Cover with a lid.

6   When ready, remove the fish from the oven and divide between plates. Spoon over the lemon, caper and butter sauce.

Octopus with caper berries, paprika and parsley

Ingredients:

2 kg | 71 oz fresh or frozen octopus, defrosted if frozen
250 ml | 9 fl oz | 1 cup olive oil
2 tbsp extra-virgin olive oil
1 lemon, cut into wedges
3 tbsp caper berries
1 tbsp smoked paprika
1 handful flat-leaf parsley, chopped
sea salt
freshly ground black pepper

Prep time: 10 minutes
Cook time: 75 minutes
Makes: 4 servings

1   Fill a large saucepan with water. Salt and bring to a rolling boil over a high heat.

2   Add the octopus to the water and reduce to a steady simmer. Cook for 45 minutes, turn the octopus over, and cook for a further 20–30 minutes until tender.

3   Remove from the water and let cool on a chopping board. Once cool, cut the tentacles into 1 cm | ½" rounds; discard the head.

4   Heat the olive oil in a heavy-based frying or sauté pan to 82°C | 180F, using a thermometer to accurately gauge the temperature.

5   Working in two batches, fry the octopus for 3 minutes. Remove to a plate lined with kitchen paper with a slotted spoon.

6   Arrange the octopus on a serving plate and drizzle with extra-virgin olive oil and a squeeze of lemon juice.

7   Scatter the caper berries on top and sprinkle with smoked paprika. Garnish with chopped parsley and serve with lemon wedges on the side.

Baked feta cheese with sun-dried tomato and capers

Ingredients:

150 g | 5 oz | 1 cup cherry tomatoes, halved

80 g | 3 oz | ½ cup sun-dried tomatoes, in oil, drained and chopped

2 tbsp baby capers, rinsed

1 clove garlic, minced

1 tbsp basil, torn

2 tsp oregano, torn

1 tbsp olive oil

freshly ground black pepper

240 g | 8 oz feta

crusty bread, to serve

Cook time: 10 minutes

Prep time: 25 minutes

Makes: 4 servings

1   Preheat the oven to 200°C (180° fan) | 400F | gas 6.

2   Stir together the cherry tomatoes, sun-dried tomatoes, capers, garlic, herbs, olive oil and some black pepper to taste in a small baking dish.

3   Place the feta in the dish and spoon over some of the tomato mixture.

4   Bake until the feta is soft and starting to colour, about 20–25 minutes.

5   Remove from the oven and let cool briefly before serving with crusty bread on the side.

Salsa verde

Ingredients:

3 tbsp baby capers, rinsed
2 tbsp pitted green olives, in brine, drained
2 tbsp gherkins, in vinegar, drained
2 cloves garlic, chopped
1 small bunch flat-leaf parsley, roughly chopped
1 handful mint leaves, chopped
1 small handful dill, chopped
1 lemon, juiced

75 ml | 2 ½ fl oz | ⅓ cup extra-virgin olive oil
2 tbsp water
sea salt
freshly ground black pepper

Prep time: 10 minutes
Makes: 4 servings

1   Combine the capers, olives, gherkins, garlic, herbs and lemon juice in a food processor. Blend on high until very finely chopped.

2   Add the olive oil and water, pulsing until just incorporated. Season to taste with salt and pepper. Cover and chill until ready to serve.

Tips
Salsa verde is a versatile green sauce that can be used to perk up a variety of meals. Serve with fish (p. 160), steamed vegetables or even spooned over a hearty lentil stew (p. 337).

The Aubergine
Symbol of Sensitivity

The dark, silky aubergine (also known as an eggplant) approaches the world with few defences: its pulpy, delicate flesh is tender; its skin easily pricked or cut. We don't need a blender to crush it. We've probably had some unappealing experiences around the aubergine. But treated carefully, it can be coaxed into something beguiling: fried in the right way, it becomes crispy and smoky; baked, it acquires richness and depth.

In humans, sensitivity is an ambivalent virtue: we can be too easily touched and moved; we can be upset by things that would be better brushed off; we are bothered because a hotel room is the wrong shape or a mattress not ideally sprung. However, our vulnerability is also, paradoxically, a source of strength. Our sensitivity allows us to notice faint tremors of interest; it provides the material around which friendship can be constructed; it draws us to nature and beauty.

Like sensitivity, the aubergine needs to be bolstered by something more robust and direct – the rich savouriness of miso, the smokiness of an open flame, or the sweetness of honey. It awaits our careful handling and judicious juxtapositions.

Recipes:
Glazed miso aubergines 60
Baba ghanoush 61
Crisp-fried aubergine with
spiced honey 62

Glazed miso aubergine

Ingredients:

2 large aubergines
1 tbsp vegetable oil
75 g | ⅓ cup white miso paste
1 tbsp fresh ginger, peeled and minced
2 tsp sesame oil
1 tsp gluten-free soy sauce
1 tsp distilled vinegar
½ tsp soft brown sugar
¼ tsp freshly ground black pepper
2 tbsp sesame seeds
1 handful coriander, to garnish

Prep time: 10 minutes
Cook time: 20 minutes
Makes: 4 servings

1   Preheat the oven to 220°C (200° fan) | 425F | gas 7.

2   Cut the aubergines in half. Score a criss-cross pattern into their flesh using the tip of a sharp knife.

3   Arrange on a baking tray lined with greaseproof paper. Brush the flesh with the vegetable oil.

4   Roast until tender, 20–25 minutes, turning once. Remove from the oven and preheat the grill to hot.

5   Whisk together the miso paste, ginger, sesame oil, soy sauce, vinegar, sugar and pepper in a small bowl until the sugar has dissolved.

6   Brush the mixture over the flesh of the roasted aubergines. Flash under the hot grill until golden-brown and lightly charred at the edges, 3–5 minutes.

7   Remove from the grill and garnish with a sprinkle of sesame seeds and some coriander before serving.

Baba ghanoush

Ingredients:

1 large aubergine
1 tbsp olive oil
1 clove garlic, crushed
1 lemon, juiced
pinch ground cumin
1 ½ tbsp tahini
1 tbsp extra-virgin olive oil
2 tbsp pine nuts
2 tbsp flat-leaf parsley, chopped

½ tsp smoked paprika
sea salt and freshly ground black
pepper

Prep and cook time: 35 minutes
Makes: 4 servings

1   Preheat the grill to hot. Cut the aubergine into ½ cm | ¼" thick slices and sprinkle with salt. Place in a colander in the sink and leave for 10 minutes.

2   After 10 minutes, pat the slices dry with kitchen paper. Arrange on a large baking tray and drizzle with olive oil, seasoning with salt and pepper at the same time.

3   Grill for 6–8 minutes, turning occasionally, until golden and lightly charred. Remove from the grill and wraps the slices in a sheet of aluminium foil. Leave to cool for 5 minutes.

4   Remove the skin from the aubergine after 5 minutes and roughly chop the flesh. Combine in a food processor with the garlic, lemon juice, cumin and tahini, and blend on high for 1–2 minutes until smooth and creamy. Season to taste as needed.

5   Spread the mixture on a serving plate and garnish with the extra-virgin olive oil, pine nuts, parsley and smoked paprika.

Crisp-fried aubergine with spiced honey

Ingredients:

2 large aubergines, trimmed and cut into ½ cm | ¼" thick slices
1 tbsp sea salt
600 ml | 21 fl oz | 2 ½ cups milk
500 ml | 18 fl oz | 2 cups vegetable oil, for frying
125 g | 4 ½ oz | 1 cup plain flour
4 tbsp honey
2 pinches cayenne pepper
1 pinch ground cinnamon

Prep and cook time: 50 minutes
Chill time: 2 hours
Makes: 4 servings

1   Place the aubergine slices in a single layer on a wire rack set over a large rimmed baking tray. Sprinkle with the salt.

2   Top with another baking tray and weigh down with baking weights, evenly distributed across the top of the tray. Let stand for 20 minutes.

3   Press down on the top tray to help release the juices from the aubergine. Transfer the slices to a large bowl and cover with the milk. Cover and chill for at least 2 hours or overnight.

4   Heat the oil to 180°C | 356F in a heavy-based casserole dish or sauté pan, using a thermometer to accurately gauge the temperature.

5   Place the flour in a shallow dish and season with a little salt. Remove the aubergine from the milk and let the excess drip off before adding to the flour, turning to coat.

6   Working in batches, fry the aubergine in the hot oil until golden-brown and crisp, turning a few times, about 3–4 minutes.

7   Transfer to a tray lined with kitchen paper to drain, covering loosely with aluminium foil to keep warm.

8   When ready to serve, gently warm the honey with the cayenne pepper and cinnamon in a small saucepan set over a low heat.

9   Arrange the aubergine slices on a serving platter and drizzle the spiced honey over them.

Mint
Symbol of Intelligence

It is hard to summarise what intelligence is like, but to take one synesthetic shortcut through the subject, one might simply say it is a little like mint.

The most intelligent teacher or writer is not the one who knows most, but who best grasps how to make us understand and take an interest in the points they wish to convey. Their merits are essentially sharpness and clarity. They take what seems complicated and vague and turn it into something precise and clear.

Mint is the sensuous equivalent of clarity and precision. The idea of intelligence enjoys great prestige, but, ironically, the prestige often attaches to its least helpful sides. We're liable to want to demonstrate our intellect by being overly wordy, by revealing the elaborate extent of our knowledge, by making convoluted arguments and drawing superfine distinctions. We pile facts and ideas on top of each other; we don't bother to explain central points that others don't yet comprehend; we do battle with unseen opponents.

Mint tells us something fundamental: the mark of deep thinking is clear and enunciated ideas. Its cool, refreshing taste evokes the ideal operations of a deft mind.

Recipes:

Melon, mint and pancetta

Ingredients:
½ ripe cantaloupe melon
1 tbsp white balsamic vinegar, or
balsamic vinegar
2 tbsp mint leaves, finely sliced
175 g | 6 oz very thin cured pancetta
slices, see Tips
sea salt
freshly ground black pepper

Prep time: 10 minutes
Makes: 4 servings

1   Cut away the peel from the melon using a sharp knife. Scoop out any seeds and stringy white pulp with a spoon.

2   Cut the melon into eight thin wedges and then cut across each wedge into two pieces. Transfer to a large mixing bowl and add the vinegar, mint and a generous pinch of salt and pepper to taste, tossing to combine.

3   Wrap the melon with pancetta slices, tearing them to size as needed. Serve immediately for best results.

Tips
Parma ham (prosciutto) would be a good alternative to thinly sliced cured pancetta.

Courgettes with mint and ricotta

Ingredients:

1 tbsp unsalted butter
2 tbsp olive oil
1 clove garlic, crushed
4 courgettes, cut into ½ cm | ¼" thick rounds
½ lemon, juice and zest, finely grated
100 g | 3 ½ oz ricotta
1 large handful of mint leaves, torn

Prep time: 5 minutes
Cook time: 10 minutes
Makes: 4 servings

1   Melt the butter with the olive oil in a large frying or sauté pan set over a moderate heat until hot.

2   Add the garlic and fry for 30 seconds. Add the courgettes in a single layer and cook over a slightly reduced heat until coloured underneath, about 5 minutes. Flip and cook for a further 2 minutes.

3   Stir in the lemon juice and about half the lemon zest. Season to taste with salt and pepper.

4   Turn out onto a serving plate and top with dollops of ricotta. Garnish with the mint and remaining lemon zest before serving.

Pea and mint soup

Ingredients:
3 tbsp butter
1 leek, finely chopped
1 litre chicken bone broth, or good
quality vegetable stock if preferred
300 g | 2 cups frozen peas, defrosted
100 g | 3 cups fresh spinach, chopped
200 ml | 7 fl oz | ⅞ cup double cream
1 handful mint leaves, chopped
¼ tsp ground nutmeg

Prep time: 5 minutes
Cook time: 15 minutes
Makes: 4 servings

1   Heat the butter in a saucepan and fry the leek for 8 minutes over a low heat.

2   Add the bone broth or stock and simmer for 5 minutes. Add the peas and spinach and cook until the spinach has wilted.

3   Stir in 150 ml | ⅔ cup of the cream, the mint and the nutmeg, then blend until smooth in a liquidiser or with a stick blender.

4   Season to taste with salt and pepper, then pour into mugs or bowls. Drizzle with the rest of the cream and add an extra grind of black pepper before serving.

Moroccan mint tea

Ingredients:

1 tbsp loose gunpowder green tea
1 large bunch of fresh mint leaves
1 litre water
3 tbsp sugar

Prep time: 5 minutes
Makes: 4–6 servings

1   Boil the water and then pour 250 ml | 1 cup into a teapot with the tea. Swirl gently to warm the pot and rinse the tea. Strain, reserving the water in a cup for later use.

2   Repeat the process but this time discard the water.

3   Place the fresh mint, sugar and the cup of water from step 1 back into the teapot. Pour in the remaining hot water. Let the tea steep for 3–4 minutes before pouring into individual glasses.

Honey
Symbol of Kindness

An odd thing about honey is that, despite being sweet, it is remarkably non-addictive. We might have to stop ourselves eating too much chocolate or ice cream, but with honey a small amount almost always seems to be enough.

This suggests that what honey brings us isn't simply pleasing; it is properly nutritious. When we secure what we really need, we normally stop desiring without end. We over-eat and over-indulge only when what we're seeking deep down isn't available. Our addiction is evidence of an ongoing chasm.

It is no coincidence that the name of this precious food is the word that lovers use when referring to the person they most prize and find comfort in. Honey seems the olfactory equivalent of kindness, as well as what we most urgently require when we are depleted and at wits' end.

Behind so many of our outward achievements, one can read, in one way or another, an attempt to get at what we pine for: the kindness of others. We strive to impress, make money and charm because we long to be treated nicely. If we could only get what we wanted more directly, we might stop much of our debilitating and futile frenzy.

In its satiating goodness, honey is an apt symbol for the kindness that we long for, but too often fail to recognise that we crave.

Recipes:
Honey madeleines 72
Manchego with honey and thyme dressing 73
Loukoumades 74
Honey soy salmon 75

Honey madeleines

Ingredients:
2 medium eggs
100 g | 1 cup icing sugar, sifted
1 tbsp clear honey
½ tsp vanilla extract
100 g | ⅔ cup plain flour, sifted
½ tsp baking powder
pinch of salt
125 g | ½ cup unsalted butter, melted
and cooled

Prep time: 10 minutes
Cook time: 10 minutes
Makes: 24 approx.

1   Pre-heat the oven to 180°C (160° fan) | 350F | gas 4. Grease two 12 hole madeleine trays with a little of the butter.

2   Beat together the eggs, icing sugar, honey and vanilla extract in a large mixing bowl with an electric hand-held whisk until thick and shiny.

3   Add the flour to the mixture in four even additions, folding in gently. Once all the flour has been folded in, fold in the baking powder and salt, followed by the melted butter until incorporated.

4   Spoon into the moulds, leaving them about three-quarters full with the batter. Bake for 12–14 minutes until golden and risen.

5   Remove and allow them to cool in the trays for a few minutes before turning out onto a wire rack to finish cooling. Serve warm or cold.

Manchego with honey and thyme dressing

Ingredients:
2 tbsp unsalted butter
1 small bunch thyme sprigs, leaves stripped
100 g | 3 ½ oz honey
300 g | 11 oz manchego, divided into four portions
crusty bread, to serve

Prep and cook time: 10 minutes
Makes: 4 servings

1   Melt the butter in a small frying pan set over a medium heat.

2   Add the thyme and sauté in the butter until fragrant, about 30–45 seconds. Stir in the honey and bring to a gentle simmer, stirring.

3   Divide the manchego between serving plates and spoon over the honey and thyme sauce. Serve with crusty bread on the side.

Loukoumades (deep-fried dough balls with honey and cinnamon)

Ingredients:

10 g fresh yeast, or 3.5 g dried yeast
100 ml | 7 tbsp lukewarm milk
250 g | 1 ⅔ cup plain (all-purpose) flour
1 tbsp honey
1 egg
40 g | ¼ cup melted butter
vegetable oil, for deep-frying
sugar, for tossing

For the syrup:

100 g | ⅓ cup honey
60 g | ¼ cup sugar

To serve:

40 g | ½ cup chopped almonds
ground cinnamon
vanilla ice cream, if desired

Prep and cook time: 1 hour
Rising time: 1 hour approx.
Makes: 4 servings

1   Dissolve the yeast in the milk. Sieve the flour into a bowl, make a well and pour in the yeast mix. Stir in the honey, cover, and leave for 30 minutes.

2   Add the egg, a pinch of salt and half the melted butter. Work to form a smooth dough that comes away from the edge of the bowl. Cover and leave to rise for a further 30 minutes.

3   Heat the oil to 180°C | 350F in a heavy-based saucepan. Knead the dough again briefly. Dip a tablespoon in the remaining butter and use it to scoop out small balls of dough. Carefully transfer to the hot oil and fry in batches for 2–3 minutes until golden brown. Remove from the oil and drain on kitchen paper.

4   For the syrup: Bring the honey and sugar to the boil with 3–4 tablespoons water and simmer for 3–4 minutes. Remove from the heat and leave to cool.

5   To serve: Arrange the dough balls on plates. Pour over the honey sauce and sprinkle with almonds and cinnamon. Serve with vanilla ice cream, if desired.

Honey soy salmon

Ingredients:
75 g | 2 ½ oz honey
60 ml | 2 fl oz dark soy sauce
2 tbsp rice wine vinegar
¼ tsp red chilli flakes (optional)
3 tbsp sunflower oil, divided
4 salmon fillets, pin-boned, patted dry
with kitchen paper
2 cloves garlic, finely chopped
1 small handful coriander, to garnish
1 tbsp sesame seeds
sea salt
freshly ground black pepper

Prep and cook time: 20 minutes
Makes: 4 servings

1   Whisk together the honey, soy sauce, vinegar and chilli flakes (if using) in a mixing bowl.

2   Heat 2 tablespoons of sunflower oil in a large non-stick frying or sauté pan set over a medium heat until hot. Season the salmon with salt and pepper.

3   Add the salmon fillets, skin side facing up, and cook until golden-brown underneath, about 5–7 minutes.

4   Carefully flip and add the remaining oil and then the garlic, cooking for 1 minute. Pour the prepared sauce from step 1 around the salmon, letting it bubble and reduce by about one-third.

5   Remove from the heat and garnish with coriander and sesame seeds. Serve straight from the pan. Serve with white rice and/or steamed greens.

The Pistachio
Symbol of Patience

We typically meet the woody, creamy pistachio in what seem like less than ideal circumstances. Its goodness is elusive, encased in a tough shell that can only be prised open, with pain and occasional risk, by inserting the end of a fingernail into an often almost invisible slit. When we finally reach our quarry, the reward is outstanding (the flavour tantalising, a touch milky) but the dose is small. Our lust for another is tempered by the knowledge of the fiddly process we will have to go through all over again.

Kindly, or just commercially minded, people have tried to rescue us from our discomfort. Brilliant engineers have designed machines to skin the shells off thousands of pistachios every minute. Large bags of naked pistachio nuts can be purchased at a modest price. We have freed ourselves from the previous speed limit of our bare hands.

But, as in so many other areas of contemporary life, we have had to pay a high price for our ingenious abundance. We can now eat twelve nuts in a minute – perhaps more; a bag can disappear while we take in a news bulletin. We expand – and grow unappreciative, too.

In its natural state, the pistachio argues against this kind of unfair and debilitating ease. It makes a case for patience, for the virtue of striving steadily, and enjoying the reward that will eventually be our due. Patience sounds like the saddest of virtues, but it has its own glory. It builds on the vital insight that getting what we want right now is often not the best outcome for us, and that we should recruit one part of our minds to stick tenaciously at working on the obstacles to our desires. The pistachio takes us solemnly back to the virtue of patience.

Recipes:

Pistachio pralines

Ingredients:

200 g | 7 oz dark brown soft sugar
225 g | 8 oz caster sugar
120 ml | 4 fl oz double cream
2 tbsp butter
1 tsp vanilla extract
200 g | 7 oz unsalted pistachios,
shelled
flaked sea salt, e.g. Maldon or fleur de
sel

Prep and cook time: 20 minutes
Cooling time: 30 minutes
Makes: 12 servings

1   Combine both sugars with the cream and butter in a heavy-based saucepan. Cook over a moderate heat, stirring, until the mixture comes to the boil.

2   Continue cooking without stirring until the mixture registers 115°C | 235F on a sugar thermometer.

3   Remove from the heat and whisk continuously for 3 minutes. Stir in the vanilla extract and pistachios.

4   Grease and line a large baking tray with greaseproof paper. Spoon about 2 tablespoons of the mixture per praline onto the paper, spaced apart.

5   Sprinkle with a little flaked sea salt and let cool until set, about 30 minutes, before serving.

Baklava

Ingredients:

250 g | 2 cups butter
450 g | 3 cups shelled pistachio nuts
12 sheets of filo pastry (2 × 270g packets)
125 ml | 1 cup water
250 g | 1 ¼ cups granulated or caster sugar
juice of ½ lemon, more to taste

Prep time: 40 minutes
Cook time: 1 hour 5 minutes
+ extra for cooling
Makes: 1 tray, approx. 36 pieces

1   Preheat oven to 180°C (160° fan) | 350F | gas 4.

2   In a food processor, pulse the pistachios until coarsely ground.

3   Melt the butter in a pan over a low heat. Brush the inside of a baking tray with a little of the melted butter. Place 1 piece of filo on the bottom, brushing with butter. Layer 5 more filo sheets on top, brushing each sheet with butter.

4   Spread pistachios on the filo in an even layer, then top with remaining filo, again brushing each sheet with butter.

5   Cut through the baklava layers to make diamond pieces before placing in the oven. Bake baklava until the top is golden brown (approx. 1 hour).

6   While the pastry is baking prepare the sugar syrup. Combine sugar with 125 ml | 1 cup of water in a pot. Bring to a boil, then let simmer for 10 minutes, until slightly thickened. Stir in lemon juice. Set aside until cool.

7   Remove the baked baklava from the oven and turn the temperature up to 200°C (180° fan) | 400F | gas 6. Pour the cooled sugar syrup over the pastry and put back in the oven for 5 minutes. Remove and leave to cool. Serve at room temperature.

Pistachio sponge cake with cream cheese frosting

Ingredients:

For the cake:

120 g | ½ cup unsalted butter, softened
350 g | 1 ½ cups caster sugar
2 large eggs
2 tsp vanilla extract
125 g | ½ cup sour cream
220 g | 1 ½ cups plain flour
1 tsp baking powder
¼ tsp bicarbonate of soda
1 pinch salt
3 tbsp milk
175 g | 1 ½ cups shelled pistachios

For the frosting:

120 g | ½ cup unsalted butter, softened
120 g | ½ cup cream cheese, softened
250 g | 2 cups icing sugar
½ tsp vanilla extract
hot water

To serve:

3 tbsp shelled pistachios, sliced
2 tbsp shelled pistachios, crushed

Prep and cook time: 1 hour 25 minutes
Makes: 8 servings

1   For the cake: Preheat the oven to 180°C (160° fan) | 350F | gas 4.
Grease and line a 900 g | 2 lb loaf tin with greaseproof paper.

2   Cream together the butter with two-thirds of the caster sugar in a large
mixing bowl until pale and fluffy, about 3 minutes.

3   Slowly beat in the eggs, one by one, and then the vanilla extract and sour
cream.

4   Stir in the flour, baking powder, bicarbonate of soda, salt, and then the
milk until you have a smooth batter. Set aside.

5   Process the pistachios with the remaining caster sugar in a food processor,
pulsing until mealy.

6   Spoon half of the batter into the prepared tin. Top with an even layer
of the pistachio mixture followed by the remaining batter.

7   Bake for about 50–60 minutes until golden and risen; a cake tester should
come out virtually clean from the centre. Remove to a wire rack to cool.

8   For the frosting: Once the cake is cool, prepare the frosting. Beat the butter
with the cream cheese in a mixing bowl until pale and creamy, 3 minutes.

9   Beat in the icing sugar in four additions until fully incorporated.
Beat in the vanilla extract and enough hot water to thin out to a pipeable
consistency. Spoon into a piping bag fitted with a round nozzle.

10 To serve: Turn out the cooled cake onto a platter. Pipe rows of the cream
cheese frosting on top. Scatter the sliced and crushed pistachios on top
before slicing and serving.

The Mushroom
Symbol of Pessimism

We may be reluctant to give the mushroom much of a role in our diet. It is disconcertingly associated with poison and goblins; it flourishes in damp, gloomy places. It grows around dying things. It might carve out its life under a fallen tree, far away from the sun. It seems aligned with sadness. Whatever time of the year we happen to be eating it, the mushroom has an autumnal quality: it speaks to us of cold, grey, rainy afternoons, the end of the year and the presence of mortal matters.

The taste of a mushroom, when cooked, is the equivalent of a sad key in music, like the introverted, melancholy tones of B minor. It's probably not something children would relish. But the mushroom begins to impress us when the more obvious pleasures of existence have lost some of their charm.

To love mushrooms is to talk to ourselves about the wisdom of pessimism: we, like they, live amid decay and darkness; the brighter pleasures will fade; we'll grow old; we'll see many of our hopes go to waste; we'll bring trouble and pain into the lives of those we most care about; the world won't appreciate our best potential. All this we have to accept. At the same time, we can still flourish. Far from being destroyed by its dank habitat, the mushroom survives. It absorbs nutrients in unpromising places; it becomes savoury and – treated the right way – a source of pleasure. The mushroom is an edible treatise on the oddity of existence.

Recipes:
Mushroom pâté 84
King oyster scallops 86
Soy-glazed shiitake mushrooms 87

Mushroom pâté

Ingredients:

2 tbsp unsalted butter

3 tbsp olive oil, divided

2 cloves garlic, finely chopped

2 shallots, finely chopped

3 thyme sprigs

450 g | 16 oz mixed wild mushrooms, cleaned, trimmed and roughly chopped

3 tbsp dry sherry, e.g. fino

1 handful flat-leaf parsley, chopped

2 tbsp cream cheese

1 tbsp lemon juice

crusty bread, or crackers, to serve

sea salt

freshly ground black pepper

Prep and cook time: 30 minutes

Chill time: 2 hours

Makes: 4 servings

1   Melt the butter with 2 tablespoons olive oil in a frying or sauté pan set over a medium heat.

2   Add the garlic, shallot and a pinch of salt, sweating until softened, about 5 minutes. Add the thyme sprigs and continue cooking for 1 minute.

3   Stir in the mushrooms and remaining oil. Increase the heat to moderate and cook until the liquid released by the mushrooms has almost entirely evaporated, about 5–7 minutes.

4   Stir in the sherry and some salt and pepper to taste. Cook over a reduced heat until the sherry has almost entirely evaporated, about 6–8 minutes.

5   Transfer the contents of the pan to a food processor, discarding the thyme. Cover and pulse several times until finely chopped.

6   Add the parsley, cream cheese and lemon juice, pulsing a few times to incorporate. Season to taste with more salt and pepper as needed.

7   Turn out into a serving bowl and smooth the top flat. Cover and chill for 2 hours.

8   When ready, serve with crusty bread or crackers on the side.

King oyster scallops

Ingredients:

4 king oyster mushroom stems, rinsed and cut into 4 cm | 1 ½" sections
1 tbsp sunflower oil
1 tbsp unsalted butter
1 small handful soft green herbs, e.g. tarragon, parsley, etc. , torn
sea salt

Prep and cook time: 10 minutes
Makes: 4 servings

1   Pat the mushroom stems dry with kitchen paper. Season with salt and pepper all over.

2   Heat the oil in a large frying or sauté pan set over a high heat until very hot.

3   Working quickly, carefully arrange the mushroom stems in the pan. Let cook until golden-brown underneath, about 1–2 minutes.

4   Flip and then add the butter to the pan, letting it melt and foam before basting it over the mushrooms with a tablespoon for about 1–2 minutes until the mushrooms are very tender.

5   Remove from the pan and garnish with some herbs before serving.

Soy-glazed shiitake mushrooms

Ingredients:

80 g | 3 oz dried shiitake mushrooms
70 ml | 2 ½ fl oz dark soy sauce
1 tbsp soft light brown sugar
2 tsp sesame seeds
2 pinches red chilli flakes (optional)

Prep and cook time: 10 minutes
Makes: 4 servings

1   Combine the mushrooms with the soy sauce, sugar and 250 ml | 1 cup water in a saucepan.

2   Bring to the boil over a moderate heat. Reduce to a gentle simmer and cover with a lid, cooking until the mushrooms are tender and have absorbed the sauce, about 15 minutes.

3   Transfer from the pan to a serving plate and sprinkle with sesame seeds and chilli flakes, if using. Serve with steamed white rice.

The Walnut
Symbol of Self-Knowledge

The walnut bears an uncanny resemblance to the human brain. It also allows us to consider the challenges and importance of getting to know our own minds.

Socrates, the earliest and greatest of Western philosophers, summed up the purpose of philosophy in the simple phrase: 'know yourself'. In giving this motto such importance in his thought, Socrates was alluding to a big problem with being human: we normally don't know ourselves well – although, fatefully, we feel as if we do. The spotlight of consciousness usually shines on only a small part of what is going on inside us. We are governed by forces to which we rarely pay attention: envy, disavowed anger, buried hurt and ideas from childhood that have come to frame our outlook but that we hardly realise we possess. What is worse, from the outside, the mind looks as if it might be simple. There is little indication of the density and maddening complexity that lies within.

Like our minds, the walnut is fragile, precious and packed in a strong casing that can be accessed only with a high degree of delicate strength. Just like walnuts, a frontal attack on prising open the mind often proves counter-productive. When we assail ourselves with blunt questions: 'What is the meaning of my life?' 'Who am I?' 'What's the right job for me?' or 'Who should I be with?' our brains are often stunned and paralysed.

The walnut stands as a reminder of the determination and forensic skill required to begin to honour Socrates's injunction.

Recipes

Walnut pesto 90
Waldorf salad 91
Date and walnut loaf 92
Candied walnuts 93

Walnut pesto

Ingredients:
25 g | 1 oz basil leaves
45 g | 1 ½ oz walnuts, chopped
1 clove garlic, crushed
60 ml | 2 fl oz extra-virgin olive oil
4 tbsp Parmesan, grated
2 tbsp lemon juice
sea salt
freshly ground black pepper

Prep and cook time: 5 minutes
Makes: 4 servings

1   Pulse together the basil and walnuts in a food processor until finely chopped. Add the garlic and olive oil, processing until smooth.

2   Add the Parmesan, lemon juice and some salt and pepper to taste, pulsing until just blended.

3   Turn out into a bowl and serve immediately for best results. Can be stored in an airtight container in the fridge.

Waldorf salad

Ingredients:

55 g | ½ cup plain yoghurt
55 g | ½ cup mayonnaise
2 tbsp warm water
2 tbsp lemon juice
150 g | 1 ½ cups walnut halves
2 Braeburn apples, cored and diced
225 g | 1 ½ cups red seedless grapes
4 sticks of celery, peeled and sliced
2 heads of butter lettuce, leaves

separated
sea salt and freshly ground pepper

Prep and cook time: 15 minutes
Makes: 2 servings

1   Whisk together the yoghurt, mayonnaise, lemon juice, warm water, and seasoning in a mixing bowl.

2   Add the walnuts, apple, grapes and celery, stirring well to coat in the dressing.

3   Arrange the lettuce leaves in serving plates and top with the dressed mixture of walnuts, apples, grapes and celery.

Date and walnut loaf

Ingredients:

150 g | 5 oz | 1 cup dates, pitted and chopped
120 g | 4 oz | ½ cup butter, softened
225 g | 8 oz | 1 cup caster sugar
1 tsp bicarbonate of soda
200 g | 7 oz | 1 ½ cups plain flour
1 large egg, beaten
1 tsp vanilla extract
2 tbsp dark rum (optional)

125 g | 4 ½ oz | ¾ cup walnuts, chopped

Prep and cook time: 1 hour 20 minutes
Makes: 1 cake, approx. 8 servings

1   Preheat the oven to 180°C (160° fan) | 350F | gas 4. Grease and line the base and sides of a 900 g | 2 lb loaf tin with greaseproof paper.

2   Combine the dates with 250 ml | 1 cup water in a saucepan. Bring to the boil over a moderate heat and then stir in the butter and sugar until the sugar has dissolved.

3   Remove from the heat and stir in the bicarbonate of soda, letting the mixture cool for 10 minutes.

4   After cooling, transfer the mixture to a mixing bowl and beat in the flour, egg, vanilla extract and rum (if using) with an electric mixer. Fold the walnuts into the batter before spooning it into the prepared tin.

5   Bake the loaf until risen and dry to the touch on top, about 1 hour.

6   Remove from the oven to a wire rack to cool completely. Turn out and slice before serving.

Candied walnuts

Ingredients:
125 g | 4 ½ oz | 1 cup walnut halves
50 g | 1 ½ oz | ¼ cup sugar
1 tbsp butter
flaked sea salt, e.g. Maldon or fleur de sel

Prep and cook time: 10 minutes
Cool time: 10 minutes
Makes: 1 cup

1   Heat a non-stick pan over a medium heat.

2   Add the walnuts, sugar and butter to the pan and cook for 4–5 minutes, stirring so that the ingredients don't burn. Coat the nuts evenly with the melted sugar and butter.

3   Working quickly, tip the mixture on to a baking tray lined with greaseproof paper, separating the nuts from each other while they are still hot. Sprinkle over a little flaked sea salt if using.

4   Leave to cool and harden for about 10 minutes. Scatter over salads or simply snack on as is.

Dark Chocolate
Symbol of Self-love

Loving oneself has traditionally been seen as a problem. It shows up as vanity, excess pride, boasting and showing off. It is linked to a refusal to accept any criticism, however legitimate, and to the maddening and erroneous conviction that others are charmed by every aspect of one's character and conduct.

However, we often suffer from an opposite problem: insufficient tenderness towards ourselves, and difficulty in believing that others might like our deeper selves.

At points, our survival depends on us learning the art of self-love. Even if we know we're exaggerating, it feels good, even necessary, to indulge in the mood from time to time, possibly while lying in bed, perhaps with some dark chocolate to hand. Under the sway of self-love, we feel anew how unfair many things are, how mean people can be, and how comparatively good and kind we remain.

Self-love is an important achievement. We should imagine what things would be like if we couldn't love ourselves. If we think of a parent comforting a child, they are in effect teaching the child how to look after themselves one day. Gradually, we learn to internalise a kindly parental attitude and come to love ourselves when no one else will in the way we were once loved.

Dark chocolate is indulgent but, like self-love, it is vital within a well-balanced life.

Recipes:
Chocolate truffles 96
Flourless chocolate cake 97
Chocolate fondant pudding 98
Chocolate-dipped fruit 99

Chocolate truffles

Ingredients:

300 g | 2 cups dark (bittersweet) chocolate, chopped
250 ml double (heavy) cream
2 tbsp butter
cocoa powder, for dusting

Prep and cook time: 20 minutes
Chill time: 4 hours
Makes: 6 servings

1 Tip the chocolate into a bowl.

2 Heat the cream and butter in a pan until simmering then pour over the chocolate and stir until the chocolate has melted and is fully incorporated.

3 Now is the time to add 1-2 tablespoons of any liqueurs or flavourings if desired. Chill for about 4 hours.

4 Roll the mixture into walnut-sized balls with oiled hands. Set on a baking sheet and dust with cocoa powder. Refrigerate until needed.

Flourless chocolate cake

Ingredients:

For the cake:

200 g | 1 ¼ cups plain chocolate, (min. 70% cocoa), chopped
1 tbsp brandy
1 tbsp strong black coffee
150 g | ¾ cup caster sugar
150 g | ¾ cup unsalted butter
100 g | 1 cup ground almonds
5 eggs, separated

For the topping:

75 g plain chocolate, (min. 70% cocoa), chopped

Prep and cook time: 1 hour 15 minutes
Makes: 1 cake, 12 servings approx.

1   For the cake: heat the oven to 180°C (160° fan) 350°F gas 4. Grease a 20cm | 8" deep cake tin and line the base with non-stick baking paper.

2   Put the chocolate, brandy, coffee, sugar and butter into a large heatproof bowl and melt together over a pan of simmering (not boiling) water. Remove from the heat and stir until smooth. Allow to cool a little, then stir in the ground almonds.

3   Stir the egg yolks into the chocolate mixture.

4   Whisk the egg whites until stiff, but not dry and gently stir into the chocolate mixture.

5   Turn the mixture into the tin and bake for 35–45 minutes, depending on how squidgy you like it. Cool in the tin for 10 minutes, then place on a wire rack to cool completely.

6   For the topping: melt the chocolate in a heatproof bowl over a pan of simmering (not boiling) water. Remove from the heat and allow to cool slightly.

7   Drizzle the melted chocolate over the cake and leave to set.

Chocolate fondant pudding

Ingredients:

For the fondants:

120 g | ½ cup butter, softened, plus
extra for greasing
35 g | ¼ cup plain flour, plus extra
for dusting
200 g | 1 ⅓ cups plain chocolate,
(min. 70% cocoa), chopped
2 medium eggs
2 egg yolks
110 g | ½ cup caster sugar

To serve:

2 tbsp cocoa powder, for dusting

Prep and cook time: 40 minutes
Makes: 4 servings

1   For the fondants: Preheat the oven to 180°C (160° fan) | 350F | gas 4.
Grease four individual pudding moulds with some softened butter. Evenly coat
with flour, tapping out any excess, and arrange on a baking tray.

2   Melt the chocolate and butter in a heatproof bowl set over a half-filled
saucepan of simmering water. Stir until smooth before removing to cool
briefly.

3   Whisk together the eggs, egg yolks and sugar in a large mixing bowl until
thick and pale, about 2–3 minutes. Fold in the cooled chocolate mixture until
incorporated. Sift in the flour and gently fold through until you have a smooth
batter.

4   Divide the mixture between the pudding moulds. Bake for 14–16 minutes
until the fondants start to come away from the edges of the moulds.

5   Remove from the oven and leave to stand for 3 minutes before inverting
onto serving plates.

6   To serve: Dust the fondants with a little cocoa powder before serving.

Chocolate-dipped fruit

Ingredients:
200 g | 7 oz | 1 ½ cups dark chocolate,
chopped
1 pinch sea salt
450 g | 16 oz | 3 cups mixed fruit,
e.g. strawberries, cherries, banana
slices

Prep and cook time: 15 minutes

Makes: 4 servings

1   Line a large baking tray with parchment paper.

2   Melt the chocolate in a heatproof bowl set over a half-filled saucepan of
simmering water, stirring occasionally.

3   Once completely melted, remove from the heat and stir in the salt.

4   Dip the fruit into the melted chocolate and arrange on the parchment,
letting them set before serving.

Garlic
Symbol of Assertiveness

In principle, we accept that we cannot please everyone, but this truth often has only a weak hold on our instincts. In practice, we typically feel we have to be people-pleasers: we cannot afford to upset or disturb others. We're afraid of what might happen if we turn down a request, or don't agree with an opinion, or come up with an idea that might be out of line with the current consensus.

Garlic is a symbol of our more staunch and assertive selves. Some people find its odour repugnant; others are delighted by its expansive, spicy warmth. But garlic isn't setting out to offend. It's fated by its nature – as we as individuals may also be – to divide opinion.

Assertion is importantly different from aggression. When we're assertive, we're saying what we really mean, but without needlessly wounding other people. In being assertive, we're accepting that what we do or say might annoy another person, but we know that we don't wish to hurt. In fact, we're sorry if we do; it's just that we have to accept the risk of speaking honestly in the name of voicing the truth as we see it.

Recipes:
Wild garlic, orange and tarragon butter 102
Tarte tatin with garlic and sweet onions 103
Gai Thod Gratiem 104
Aioli 105

Wild garlic, orange and tarragon butter

Ingredients:
1 large bunch wild garlic, leaves only
1 small bunch tarragon, leaves only
1 orange, juice and zest, finely grated
250 g | 1 cup butter, softened
sea salt

Prep and cook time: 20 minutes
Chill time: 12 hours
Makes: 6–8 servings

1   Wash the garlic and tarragon leaves under cold running water. Pat dry with kitchen paper.

2   Combine the leaves, orange juice and orange zest with the butter, in a food processor. Blend on high until smooth.

3   Scrape the butter from the processor onto a sheet of greaseproof paper. Roll and shape into a cylinder, and then chill overnight before using. The butter can be spread under turkey or chicken skin before roasting, or simply melt over grilled vegetables.

Tarte tatin with garlic and sweet onions

Ingredients:

1 tsp butter

2 tbsp olive oil

4 mild red onions, cut into thin wedges

6–8 cloves garlic, roughly chopped

3–4 sprigs thyme, cut into smaller pieces

75 ml | ⅓ cup balsamic vinegar

1 pinch brown sugar

1 sheet ready-rolled puff pastry, approx. 300 g | 10 oz

Prep and cook time: 20 minutes

Cook time: 35 minutes

Makes: 1 tart (or frying pan) 22 cm diameter

1   Heat the oven to 190°C (170° fan) | 375F | gas 5. Grease a tart tin (or a cast iron frying pan) with butter.

2   Heat the oil in a frying pan and gently fry the onions, stirring occasionally, for approx. 5 minutes. Add the garlic, thyme and vinegar. Simmer gently for around 5 minutes, then season to taste with salt, ground black pepper and sugar.

3   Transfer the onions to the tin. Unroll the pastry and cut out a circle around 5 cm larger than the tin (approx. 27 cm in diameter). Place this on top of the onions and press down well into the tin around the edge. Bake in the oven for approx. 25 minutes.

4   Turn out of the tin and ideally serve hot, with a leaf salad.

Gai Thod Gratiem
(Garlic-fried chicken)

Ingredients:

8 cloves garlic, finely chopped
1 tsp freshly ground white pepper
1 ½ tbsp light soy sauce
1 ½ tbsp oyster sauce
1 ½ tbsp rice wine vinegar
1 tbsp light soft brown sugar
2 large skinless chicken breasts, cut into 3 cm | 1 ¼" cubes
75 ml | 2 ½ fl oz | ⅓ cup sunflower oil, or sunflower oil
1 red chilli, finely sliced, to garnish

Prep and cook time: 15 minutes
Chill time: 1 hour
Makes: 2 servings

1   Stir together the garlic, white pepper, soy sauce, oyster sauce, vinegar and sugar in a mixing bowl until the sugar has dissolved.

2   Add the chicken, stirring well. Cover and chill for 1 hour.

3   Heat a wok over a high heat until hot. Add the oil, swirling to coat, and then add the marinaded chicken, stir-frying until golden-brown and cooked through, about 5–7 minutes.

4   Transfer to a bowl and garnish with sliced chilli before serving with rice.

Aioli

Ingredients:
8 cloves garlic, peeled
250 ml | 1 cup extra-virgin olive oil
1 tsp lemon juice
sea salt

Prep time: 20–30 minutes
Makes: 1 cup

1   Place the garlic cloves into a mortar with a pinch of sea salt.

2   Mash the garlic into a smooth paste. Mix in the lemon juice.

3   Add the oil to the mortar a drop at a time, mashing and stirring into the garlic paste. Make sure the oil is fully incorporated before adding more. Keep going until you have the consistency of mayonnaise.

4   If the aioli gets too thick, simply add a few drops of water. Use as a dip for steamed artichoke or with a pan fried steak.

The Egg
Symbol of Compassion

Compassion for others is an attractive notion, but in reality we often find it difficult to be kindly and understanding towards people who make a lot of noise at unwanted times, frustrate our plans, tell us we're idiots when we try to help them, or who expect us to pay for everything. Unless, of course, they are small children, only recently hatched from their eggs.

One of the striking things about compassion is that we rarely withhold it from anyone aged 4 or under. We usually forgive a 2-year-old for things we would resent in an adult.

We generally accept the idea that children deserve the kindest interpretation of their actions: they are simply tired, confused or hungry. We grasp that they don't easily understand good intentions; they get swamped by panic; their emotions are more powerful than their reason. We don't become vengeful or righteous around small children's annoying tendencies.

However, the extenuating, compassionate grounds we allow in our dealings with children apply around adults as well. Adults, too, get derailed by fear and anxiety; their moods are equally subject to bodily states; they too lash out and say things they don't really mean; they too turn their frustration on innocent bystanders because of a compelling need to find someone to blame. We know this not because of a detailed examination of other people's minds, but because we recognise that this is a fair assessment of our own behaviour.

A great source of compassion, therefore, comes from our ability to remember that the difficult other was once a baby and, (like everyone), has only imperfectly developed into an adult. Much of their mind was formed when they sat in a high chair; their emotional patterns were laid down when they were baffled by the task of tying a pair of shoe laces; they were strongly influenced by their parents, long before they had any capacity to choose their own company. When we look at a photo of someone as a child, we're almost always moved to see them in a new light. The childhood state doesn't just represent a long-surpassed phase; it captures a significant part of who this person still is. To a significant degree, they are still the person they were when they had a fringe and braces. If only we could keep this thought at the front of our minds, our view of their failings would change dramatically.

The egg is the universal symbol of origins. It comes in many forms: the grand duck egg, the familiar chicken egg, the exciting dinosaur egg, the fragile quail egg, or the ultra-tough ostrich egg. But all these eggs point us in the same direction. However different the adult appears, it always shared this same strange, modest, endearing starting point. Not everyone's childhood was the same, but everyone was a child once.

By contemplating the egg of a *Tyrannosaurus rex* in a museum, we may even find ourselves feeling a little more tender and sympathetic towards this aggressive and terrifying adult. Once, they were tiny and vulnerable; the potential victim of their own later prey. Similarly, the bullying, mean person was also once a small baby: they had to be spoon-fed; they needed someone to sing them to sleep at night; they were easily frightened; they didn't choose their own beginnings.

adjustment. However difficult or obnoxious this person may be, they were also once a human egg; an innocent embryo. When they were born, they were tiny and dependent; they wanted to be loved; they cried easily; they clutched a corner of a soft blanket for comfort; they knew nothing. Once, possibly, they sat in a highchair with a bib around their neck, and someone broke open the top of a soft-boiled egg, placed it in an egg cup and praised them for dipping a finger of toast into the runny yolk. We might imagine that this woman is again seeing this universal child behind the gruff individual feeling sorry for themselves in the room next door.

Jean-Baptiste-Siméon Chardin, *Meal for a Convalescent*, c. 1747.

Offering, or eating, an egg is a route to kindness. In a profoundly loving picture, the 18th-century French artist Chardin shows a woman taking the top off a boiled egg. She's preparing a meal for someone who hasn't been well. Maybe it's for her overbearing employer or her far-from-perfect husband. But in her contemplation of the egg it feels as if she's making a powerful emotional

Recipes:

French omelette 109
Shakshuka 110
Pastel de Nata 111

French omelette

Ingredients:
12 large free-range eggs
4 tbsp unsalted butter, cubed
1 handful chives, finely chopped
(optional)
sea salt
freshly ground black pepper

Prep and cook time: 15 minutes
Makes: 4 servings

1   For each omelette, beat together three eggs with plenty of salt and pepper in a mixing bowl.

2   Melt 1 tablespoon butter in a non-stick omelette or frying pan set over a moderate heat until hot.

3   Add the beaten egg to the pan, letting it spread out and set underneath before drawing the sides inwards to let the uncooked egg run underneath.

4   Once the omelette is golden-brown underneath, fold the omelette over and slide out onto a serving plate. Repeat steps 1–3 for the remaining omelettes.

5   Serve the omelettes with a garnish of chopped chives, if desired.

Shakshuka (poached eggs in tomato sauce)

Ingredients:

3 tbsp olive oil
2 medium onions, chopped
1 red pepper, seeded and diced
1 small red chilli, seeded and diced
4 cloves garlic, finely chopped
50 g | ¼ cup tomato puree
800 g | 4 cups canned chopped tomatoes
1 bay leaf
1 tbsp caster sugar

3 tsp sweet paprika
2 tsp ground cumin
½ tsp ground caraway
4 large free-range eggs
coriander sprigs, to garnish
sea salt
freshly ground black pepper

Prep and cook time: 50 minutes
Makes: 4 servings

1   Heat the olive oil in a large sauté pan or casserole dish set over a medium heat until hot.

2   Add the onions and sauté for 6–8 minutes until softened and translucent. Add the pepper, chilli and garlic, and cook for 5 minutes, sauté stirring frequently.

3   Stir in the tomato puree and cook for a further minute. Add the chopped tomatoes, bay leaf, sugar and spices, and stir well.

4   Cook at a steady simmer for 15–20 minutes until thickened. Season to taste with salt and pepper.

5   Create four little pockets in the stew and crack the eggs into them. Cover with a lid and cook over a slightly reduced heat for 6–8 minutes until the whites are set.

6   Serve with a sprinkling of coriander and some more seasoning on top.

Pastel de nata (Portuguese custard tarts)

Ingredients:
300 g | 10 oz puff pastry
flour, for dusting
500 ml | 2 ½ cups milk
225 g | 1 cup sugar
1 tsp vanilla extract
1 tbsp cornflour (cornstarch)
1 pinch salt
ground cinnamon
2 eggs
3 egg yolks

Prep and cook time: 50 minutes
Cook time: 10 minutes
Makes: 12 tarts

1   Heat the oven to 200°C (180° fan) | 400F | gas 6. Grease a 12 hole muffin tin or 12 individual baking moulds.

2   Roll out the puff pastry on a floured surface and cut out 12 rounds, approx. 10cm | 4" diameter. Line the tins with the pastry rounds.

3   Bring the milk to a boil in a pan. Remove from the heat.

4   Mix together the sugar, vanilla and cornflour and add to the milk. Stir well and boil for 2–3 minutes to thicken slightly.

5   Remove from the heat and cool slightly. Stir in the salt, a pinch of cinnamon, the eggs and egg yolks. Divide the custard between the pastry cases.

6   Bake for 12–15 minutes. Cool completely before serving.

Rhubarb
Symbol of Appreciation

It sounds peculiar, and not a little patronising, to suggest that one of the major obstacles to contentment might lie in our failure to master the skill of appreciation. For a start, we don't tend to think that appreciation is a skill: it seems as if we are spontaneously endowed with the capacity to judge what is worth treasuring, so we must be correct in our assessment of what is worthy of gratitude. It is also natural to trust that most of what is worth treasuring is not yet in our possession.

Then, occasionally, a surprising feeling can befall us. We land on something familiar and accessible, from which we have not drawn value in years, and are overwhelmed by a sense of its importance, beauty and worth. It might be the view from the window, the way the sunlight falls on the curtain, the stillness of the evening at the top of the house, the hand of our lover as it rests on the table in front of us – or a bowl of recently cooked rhubarb. The memory of our previous neglect, combined with our new heightened awareness, pushes us to acknowledge some unknown flaws in our mechanisms of appreciation and humbly to wonder at how widely these may extend. We can end up on the cusp of a bold, huge and disturbing thought: that our dissatisfactions may be more the result of a failure to draw value from what we already have than from any absence of things of quality.

At first sight, rhubarb is unappealing and boring, which is why it is a fitting symbol of appreciation. Imperfectly cooked, it is sour, messy and disgusting. It has no prestige. One learns to despise rhubarb. But treated the right way, its charms are exemplary and manifold.

Rhubarb is a reminder of a central theme of life: the potential attraction of the overlooked element. We are already far richer than we think.

Recipes:
Rhubarb crumble 114
Rhubarb and ginger syllabub 115
Rhubarb and ricotta bread &
butter pudding 116

Rhubarb crumble

Ingredients:

For the filling:

1 tbsp butter, softened

500 g | 18 oz | 3 ½ cups rhubarb, cut into 3 cm | 1 in pieces

200 g | 7 oz | 2 cups fresh or frozen cranberries, thawed if frozen

4 tbsp caster sugar

½ orange, juiced

For the crumble:

125 g | 4 ½ oz | ½ cup caster sugar

150 g | 5 oz | 1 ½ cups rolled oats

70 g | 2 ½ oz | ⅔ cup plain flour

110 g | 4 oz | ½ cup butter, melted

Prep and cook time: 50 minutes

Makes: 4 servings

1　Heat the oven to 180°C (160° fan) | 350°F | gas 4. Grease a baking dish with 1 tablespoon butter.

2　For the filling: mix together the rhubarb, cranberries, sugar and orange juice. Put into the baking dish.

3　For the crumble: rub the ingredients together until crumbly. Sprinkle over the fruit.

4　Bake for 20–25 minutes until the rhubarb is tender and the crumble is golden. Serve warm with custard or vanilla ice cream.

Rhubarb and ginger syllabub

Ingredients:

450 g | 16 oz | 3 cups rhubarb, trimmed and cut into 2 ½ cm | 1" slices
2 tbsp fresh ginger, peeled and finely chopped
80 g | 3 oz | ⅓ cup caster sugar
100 ml | 3 ½ fl oz | 7 tbsp dry white wine
300 ml | 11 fl oz | 1 ⅓ cups whipping cream
100 g | 3 ½ oz | ½ cup mascarpone
60 g | 2 oz | ½ cup icing sugar, sifted
2 tbsp crystallised ginger, finely chopped
shortbread, to serve

Prep and cook time: 20 minutes
Makes: 4 servings

1   Combine the rhubarb, ginger, caster sugar and wine in a heavy-based saucepan. Bring to the boil over a moderate heat and then reduce to a simmer until the rhubarb has softened, about 5–7 minutes.

2   Remove from the heat and let cool.

3   In the meantime, whisk together the cream, mascarpone and icing sugar in a mixing bowl until thick and creamy.

4   Fold about one-quarter of the rhubarb mixture into the whipped cream mixture.

5   Divide the remaining rhubarb mixture between four serving glasses and top with the whipped cream mixture and a garnish of crystallised ginger. Serve with shortbread on the side.

Rhubarb and ricotta bread & butter pudding

Ingredients:

150 g | 5 oz | ⅔ cup caster sugar
450 g | 16 oz g rhubarb, trimmed and
sliced into 4 cm | 1.5" pieces
350 ml | 12 fl oz | 1 ½ cups milk
250 ml | 9 fl oz | 1 cup whipping cream
1 tsp vanilla extract
3 large eggs
1 large egg yolk
1 pinch salt
250 g | 9 oz stale brioche slices, or
stale white bread slices, see Tips
3 tbsp butter, softened
250 g | 9 oz | 1 cup ricotta, drained
2 tbsp icing sugar, plus extra for
serving
1 orange, zest only, finely grated

To serve:

single cream, or vanilla ice cream

Prep and cook time: 1 hour 25 minutes

Makes: 4–6 servings

1   Combine 100 ml | ½ cup water with 50 g | ¼ cup caster sugar in a large saucepan. Bring to the boil over a moderate heat and then stir in the rhubarb.

2   Cover and simmer over a low heat until soft, about 7–10 minutes. Transfer to a plate lined with kitchen paper to drain.

3   Combine the milk, cream and vanilla extract in a saucepan. Bring to the boil over a moderate heat. In the meantime, whisk together the eggs, egg yolk, salt and remaining sugar in a large mixing bowl until pale and thick, about 2–3 minutes.

4   Remove the milk and cream from the heat and gradually whisk into the egg mixture until incorporated.

5   Spread the brioche slices with the butter. Briefly beat the ricotta with the icing sugar and orange zest in a mixing bowl.

6   Spread it onto the brioche slices and then arrange them in an ovenproof baking dish large enough to hold the slices in overlapping layers.

7   Spoon the rhubarb on top and pour over the egg custard mixture from step 4. Let the pudding stand for 30 minutes. Preheat the oven to 180°C (160° fan) | 350F | gas 4.

8   Transfer the dish to the oven, baking the pudding until golden-brown and puffed, about 40–45 minutes.

9   Remove from the oven and let stand for at least 10 minutes before dusting with icing sugar and serving with cream or ice cream.

Tips
This recipe works best with 3-day old brioche or bread slices.

2
Looking after ourselves

Looking after ourselves

Knowing how to look after ourselves deserves to be counted as one of the great arts of life. For much of our adulthoods, there is no one else to do the task for us. We have to calm ourselves down, ensure we are getting enough sleep, regulate our excitements, do our taxes, reflate our self-esteem, lend our hopes encouragement, occasionally administer the right sort of criticism, and pick ourselves up after yet another defeat.

A lot of the nurture will involve soothing words or encouraging statements whispered by one side of the mind to the other. *You can do it. Don't listen to them. What do they know anyway? We'll work this one out ...*

However, some of the self-nurture will involve food. We'll bring ourselves down from panic and despair with the help of certain dishes. We'll simmer just the right kind of soup for a break-up. In the midst of self-hatred, we'll steer ourselves towards some new-season vegetables. We'll know to administer sugar and salt, carbohydrates and proteins, spices and marinades so as to regulate and assuage the tempests in our minds.

What follows is a range of dilemmas and pains and, in response, recipes we might prepare for ourselves when confusion and misery descend. The approach turns our kitchens into a form of psychotherapeutic chemist, adroitly dispensing food for the more complicated, sad and troubled moments of our souls.

'It's all getting too much'

A difficult work deadline looms; the second reminder letter for an unpaid bill rebukes us; a mobile phone goes missing. It doesn't take much for an otherwise manageable life to go awry, and for a sense of foreboding to gather. We need comfort. Eating can't directly solve our problems. This recipe for pasta bake can't pay the bill, find the phone or sit up late to finish the report in our stead. But what we suffer from aren't only the troubles themselves; it's the awful feeling of depletion and weakness in the face of them that really takes the toll.

That's where food can help. The right food takes the edge off panic. It rallies our flagging energies and reminds us that ordinary good things survive, despite present tensions. A pasta bake has a nursery quality that acknowledges and soothes the part of us that remains a fractious child, despite the job title, work suits, credit cards and trappings of adulthood.

Orecchiette pasta bake

Ingredients:

2 tbsp olive oil
½ large onion, finely chopped
2 cloves garlic, finely chopped
1 tsp fennel seeds
400 g | 14 oz | 2 cups tinned chopped
tomatoes
1 handful basil leaves, plus extra
to garnish
450 g | 16 oz | 4 cups orecchiette

250 g | 9 oz | 1 cup ricotta
3 tbsp Parmesan, grated
sea salt
freshly ground black pepper

Prep and cook time: 1 hour 20 minutes
Makes: 4 servings

1   Preheat the oven to 180°C (160° fan) | 350F | gas 4. Heat the olive oil in a saucepan set over a medium heat until hot. Add the onion, garlic, fennel seeds and a pinch of salt, sweating until the onion is soft, about 5–6 minutes.

2   Stir in the chopped tomatoes and basil leaves. Bring to a simmer and cook over a reduced heat for 10 minutes, stirring occasionally. Remove from the heat and season with plenty of salt and pepper. Transfer to a food processor and purée until smooth.

3   Cook the orecchiette in a large saucepan of salted, boiling water until just tender to the bite (al dente), about 10–12 minutes.

4   Drain well and return to the saucepan they were cooked in, adding the tomato sauce. Stir thoroughly to combine, seasoning to taste with more salt and pepper as needed.

5   Transfer the pasta to a baking dish. Top with ricotta and Parmesan.

6   Bake until golden-brown on top, about 25–35 minutes. Remove from the oven and let stand briefly before serving with a garnish of basil.

For the five minutes that your fingers are in the mixing bowl your chaotic day slips from view.

'I want to feel more grounded'

When you spend your day running
from A to B, and then on to C, the
thought of making bread seems far-
fetched. It's all very well for the stay-
at-homes, who have time to knead
together the ingredients and wait for
the dough to rise. But wait a minute.
What about a loaf without yeast,
that can be on the table in under
an hour? And what if it's a loaf that
never fails, is instantly gratifying, and
smells wondrous? And what if, for the
five minutes that your fingers are in
the mixing bowl, rubbing butter into
flour, your chaotic day slips from
view like the sun setting behind a hill,
leaving your feet planted firmly on
the ground?

Brown soda bread

Ingredients:
500 g | 18 oz | 3 ⅓ cups
wholemeal flour
1 tsp sea salt
1 tsp bicarbonate of soda
25 g | 2 tbsp butter
400 ml | 1 ½ cups milk
1 lemon, juiced
2 tsp honey

Prep time: 5 minutes
Cook time: 40 minutes
Makes: 1 large loaf

1   Preheat oven to 200°C (180° fan) | 400F | gas 6. Mix together the dry ingredients in a bowl. Rub in the butter.

2   Mix together the milk and lemon juice in a jug and leave to stand for a minute. Stir in the honey, and pour into the flour mix. Using a knife combine the mix into a sticky dough.

3   Tip onto a floured work surface and shape it into a round loaf, approximately 20 cm | 8" in diameter.

4   Put the loaf on a baking tray and score the top of the dough with a deep cross. Bake for 35–40 mins until the bottom of the loaf sounds hollow when tapped.

5   Cool on a wire rack. Serve warm with butter, cheese and chutney.

'I can't work it out'

Thinking our problems through is often the best thing we can do. But sometimes, we get stuck. We ruminate and obsess. The same dark and panicky thoughts preoccupy us; the same fear keeps on intruding itself. We might need to find something else to do while the mind sorts itself out in the background.

Japanese monks developed a cult of raking gravel into beautiful patterns in their temple gardens: the painstaking, physical nature of the task and the pleasing results were found to offer relief from mental agitation. The French philosopher Jacques Derrida (1930–2004) spent many of his afternoons playing snooker as an antidote to his turbulent reflections. As these routine tasks unfolded, the monks and Derrida found that their difficult thoughts gradually sorted themselves out.

The slow, meditative preparation of a risotto can offer comparable relief. It involves us in a careful but not overly exacting process that distracts the skittish, nervous part of the mind and allows our deeper, slower thinking to occur. As we coax creamy starch from the grains of rice we move away from the unhelpful notion that our best ideas are always the result of head-on thinking, sitting in a room with a blank sheet of paper. Better thoughts are more likely to strike as we pour another ladle of stock into the pot. We should keep a notepad in the kitchen.

Basic risotto

Ingredients:
2 tbsp olive oil
2 shallots, finely chopped
2 cloves garlic, minced
250 g | 9 oz | 1 ½ cups Arborio rice
175 ml | 6 fl oz | ¾ cup white wine
1500 ml | 53 fl oz | 6 cups vegetable
stock, kept hot on the stove
100 ml | 3 ½ fl oz | 7 tbsp double
cream
40 g | 1 ½ oz | ⅓ cup Parmesan, finely
grated, plus extra to serve

½ lemon, juice and zest,
finely grated
1 handful flat-leaf parsley,
finely chopped
sea salt
freshly ground black pepper

Prep and cook time: 1 hour 10 minutes
Makes: 4 servings

1   Heat the oil in a large saucepan set over a medium heat. Add the shallots, garlic and a pinch of salt, sweating for 5 minutes until softened.

2   Add the rice and cook for 2–3 minutes, stirring frequently, until translucent in appearance. Add the wine, bring to the boil, and then reduce to a simmer for a further 2 minutes.

3   Incorporate the stock by the ladleful, stirring and simmering until the rice has absorbed all the stock before adding the next ladle.

4   Continue in this fashion until the rice has absorbed all the stock and is tender to the bite and creamy; about 30 minutes – you may not need to use all the stock.

5   Once the rice is ready, stir in the cream and return to a simmer. Fold through the Parmesan and lemon zest. Adjust the seasoning to taste with salt, pepper and some lemon juice.

6   Divide between bowls or dishes and garnish with some chopped parsley and more grated Parmesan.

'I don't like myself very much ...'

Some days, we can't bear ourselves. We know so much about our errors, follies and vanity. We speak to ourselves in the harshest voices: *You little idiot, you stupid wretch ...* We are far from perfect, but, in order to keep going and summon our better efforts, we need to be fairer and nicer to ourselves. It won't do just to hurl insults across consciousness. We could try to channel the voice of a kindly relative – perhaps a grandparent who was free from the practical burden of looking after us and was aware enough of their own mortality to value modest things. They loved us purely and wanted, more than anything, for us to be happy on our own terms. We could do with summoning up this kind of voice more regularly in our present lives. Food is a powerful way of connecting us emotionally, via the senses, with a far-off, benign part of our past experience.

There will always be a strongly personal element to what foods evoke for us the kindly inner voice we need. Kindly reassurance might be associated with spaghetti bolognese or creamy fish pie, dishes that seem to whisper with tenderness: *You can do it; this isn't going to be the end; it'll look a lot better in the morning.*

Fish pie

Ingredients:

500 g | 3 ⅓ cups floury potatoes
5 tbsp butter
1 leek, sliced into rings
1 yellow pepper, finely diced
2 tbsp flour
400 ml | 1 ½ cup milk
100 g | ½ cup crème fraîche
500 g | 3 ⅓ cups fish fillet, ready to cook, e.g. salmon and cod, cut into bite-sized pieces
250 g | 1 ⅔ cups prawns, ready to cook

2 tbsp freshly chopped parsley
2 tbsp freshly chopped dill
2 tbsp lemon juice
50 g | ½ cup grated cheese, e.g. cheddar
100 ml | 7 tbsp warm milk
nutmeg

Prep time: 1 hour 10 minutes
Cook time: 35 minutes
Makes: 4 servings

1   Cook the potatoes in salted, boiling water for around 25–30 minutes.

2   Heat the oven to 200°C (180°C in a fan oven), 400°F, gas 6 and grease a casserole dish or pie dish with a little of the butter.

3   Melt 2 tablespoons butter in a saucepan and fry the leek and pepper for 2–3 minutes without browning. Stir in the flour then add the milk. Season with salt and ground black pepper and stir in the crème fraîche. Remove from the heat and season well with salt and ground black pepper.

4   Tip the fish, prawns, parsley and dill into the dish. Drizzle with lemon juice and pour over the sauce.

5   Drain the potatoes and allow the steam to evaporate, then mash well. Stir in the rest of the butter, the cheese and the warm milk. Season to taste with salt and nutmeg and spread over the fish.

6   Bake in the oven for 35 minutes until golden brown.

'My past is so full of bittersweet memories'

A lot of our past is made up of memories colloquially known as 'bittersweet': both pleasurable and a little painful. We might remember the afternoons we spent with our grandmother when we were little. Together we'd do a bit of weeding in her tiny garden, then we'd make lunch and play cards. Sometimes she showed us old photographs of her own distant childhood. We enjoyed those times, but the memory of them is mixed up with the knowledge of what happened later. In adolescence, we pushed away from her, we almost never visited, and she died before we'd found our adult selves. She never got to know about the love we now feel for her. We wince at our recollections.

Or perhaps we remember being fifteen and in love for the first time. The object of our affection was just half a year older, which seemed a lot then. We felt such tenderness and respect for them, but, crippled by shyness, never said anything. There was one ambiguous moment, at dusk, by the river. Then it passed. Recently we heard they had a child and moved north. We wonder, with pain, if we could ever feel that way about anyone now, with the same unguarded sense of hope and conviction. It seems sadly typical that we let what might have been the best person in the world slip through our fingers.

Bittersweet memories force us to acknowledge that the positive in our lives is often entwined with something more difficult. In the presence of bittersweet memories, we feel the pain of being flawed, error-prone, time-short and regretful.

It would be easier if things were more clear-cut: white is simple enough to take and black too can be coped with when we know it has to be borne. It's the grey – with its mercurial admixture of hope and regret – that is so hard to deal with. We long to call some people pure and dismiss others as monstrous, and we do the same with sections of our lives. But to be open to bittersweet memories is to accept ambivalence: a capacity to have two contrasting, opposed emotions about the same thing without disowning either. Both are important; neither can be denied. We should recognise, rather than denying, the fiendishly mixed character of experience.

There are dishes that speak to our bittersweet memories. By making them from time to time we can remind ourselves that this confusingly mixed emotion is important.

Bittersweet chocolate torte

Ingredients:
200 g | 1 cup butter
200 g | 1 cup dark chocolate, (min. 70% cocoa) chopped
4 large eggs
200 g | 1 cup caster sugar
30 ml | 2 tbsp brewed espresso, cooled to room temperature
50 g | ½ cup plain flour
50 g | ½ cup ground almonds
Cocoa powder for dusting (optional)

Prep time: 15 minutes
Cook time: 35–45 minutes
Makes: 1 × 23 cm | 9" tin, approx. 8–10 slices

1 Heat oven to 180°C (160° fan) | 350F | gas 4.

2 Grease and line a 23 cm | 9" springform cake tin with non-stick baking paper.

3 Put the butter and chocolate into small saucepan over a medium heat and melt together, stirring frequently. Set to one side.

4 In a separate bowl, beat the eggs, sugar and brewed espresso together for at least 5 minutes until thick and voluminous.

5 Gently fold the chocolate mixture into the egg mixture with a large metal spoon until completely combined.

6 Fold in the flour and almonds into the mix, again making sure everything is combined. Turn the mixture into the tin and bake for 35–45 minutes. Cool in the tin for 10 minutes, then place on a wire rack to cool completely. Dust with cocoa powder for an extra bitter hit.

'I'm in a melancholy mood'

In a busy, success-oriented world in which we're continually encouraged to stoke our ambitions and invest ourselves in new ventures, it can be shameful to feel gloomy, downcast and with a strong desire to hide under a blanket. We want to commune in imagination with the last leaves falling from a tree in early winter, or with the grey, vacant immensity of the ocean, or to immerse ourselves in songs of lamentation and regret. It's tempting to recast melancholy almost as an illness in need of medical intervention. In fact, a feeling of general sadness often makes sense.

Melancholy isn't something that needs to be cured. There is much about the human condition that is far from cheerful. Our lives are brief and filled with trouble. Relationships that start with the promise of love seem almost inevitably to lead to conflict and mutual disappointment. There is a zone of loneliness at the centre of most lives. Our best potential is rarely encouraged or rewarded by the world; those we love will suffer and die; time is running away from us; we've already squandered much of our existence. Melancholy is a legitimate, sensitive and intelligent response to the human condition.

Rather than try to suppress or evade it, we should seek to encounter it properly. There are dishes that take our melancholy seriously. They don't try to cheer us up; like an ideal friend, they seem to know and share our sorrows.

Slow cooked beef pho

Ingredients:

Broth:

1 ½ kg | 3 lb of beef shin,
1 kg | 2 lb oxtail
2 large onions, skin removed
and halved
200 g | 7 oz of root ginger, peeled
3 star anise
1 cinnamon sticks
4 cloves
1 tsp coriander seeds
50 ml | 3 tbsp fish sauce
1 tbsp soft light brown sugar

To serve:

600 g | 20 oz wide flat dried rice
noodles
4–6 spring onions, thinly sliced
2 bird's eye chillis, finely sliced
4–6 handfuls of bean sprouts
(optional)
400 g | 15 oz sirloin or fillet steak
(optional), thinly sliced
1 lime, cut into wedges
Large bunch of coriander
Large bunch of Thai basil
Sriracha, hoisin and chilli oil
(optional)

Prep time: 1 hours
Cook time: 5–6 hours
Makes 4–6 servings

1   Place the onions and ginger under a high grill, turning regularly until blackened on all sides, about 15 minutes total. Set to one side.

2   Put the beef shin and oxtail in a large pan and cover with cool water. Bring to a boil over a high heat, continue for 15 minutes. Drain water and under cool running tap water rinse the meat and pan thoroughly.

3   Return the beef shin and oxtail back into the clean pan and cover with three litres of cold water, or as much as will fit into the pan. Add the blackened onions and ginger along with the spices. Bring to a boil over a high heat and then reduce to a bare simmer. Cook uncovered for 5–6 hours, topping up with water as necessary. The meat should be soft and falling off the bone.

4   Strain through a fine mesh sieve, retaining the oxtail. Add the fish sauce, sugar, salt and black pepper to the broth to taste, and pick the meat from the oxtail.

5   Cook the noodles according to the packet instructions and divide between four to six bowls. Pour the hot broth over the noodles and garnish with spring onion, a little chilli and the bean sprouts. Place the oxtail and sliced raw beef (if using) on top.

6   Serve with the limes and remaining chilli on the side along with the herbs and condiments as desired.

'I want to be immortal'

We know we can't live forever,
and the relationship between what we
eat and how long we will live is, at
points, humblingly uncertain. But
there are certain foods that do
something almost as good as assuring
us a century on the planet: they boost
our sense of immortality. They lend us
a confident sense that we can
overcome whatever obstacles come
our way. They make us feel energetic
and bionic, as if our whole body were
an advanced machine reliably in the
command of our will. If these foods
are a little unpleasant or daunting,
all the better for it. We work with a
well-established association in our
minds between what is good for us
and what makes us suffer. But this is
the best sort of suffering – suffering in
the name of (apparently) staying
alive forever. If there were angels, and
they got peckish, this is what they
might have for lunch.

Barley salad with sugar snap peas

Ingredients:

200 g | 7 oz | 1 cup pearl barley
250 g | 9 oz | 2 cups sugar snap peas
3 tbsp lemon juice
1 ½ tsp Dijon mustard
¼ tsp caster sugar
1 handful tarragon, finely chopped
75 ml | 2 ½ fl oz | ⅓ cup extra-virgin olive oil
½ cucumber, diced

80 g | 3 oz | ½ cup feta, crumbled (optional)
sea salt
freshly ground black pepper

Prep and cook time: 1 hour 10 minutes
Makes: 4 servings

1   Place the pearl barley in a heavy-based saucepan and stir in 600 ml | 2 ½ cups water and 1 tsp salt. Bring to the boil and then reduce to a simmer.

2   Cover and cook over a low heat until the barley is tender to the bite, about 45–50 minutes.

3   When ready, drain and let cool for 10 minutes.

4   In the meantime, place the sugar snap peas in steaming basket. Cover and steam over a half-filled saucepan of simmering water until tender, about 3–4 minutes. Remove from the heat.

5   Whisk together the lemon juice, mustard, sugar and a pinch of salt and pepper to taste in a large mixing bowl until the sugar and salt have dissolved. Stir in the tarragon and then gradually whisk in the olive oil.

6   Add the barley, peas and cucumber to the bowl of dressing, stirring and tossing to combine. Season to taste with salt and pepper as needed.

7   Divide between bowls and garnish with crumbled feta if using.

'Tomorrow will be challenging'

Yes, it will be. And the heart starts to
sink. There's something awkward to
deal with – an unpleasant meeting at
work; the pain of doing a tax return; a
confrontation with an ex who wants to
have something out with us; a heap of
things we've been putting off and we
really have to get on with ...

Food can't make any of these things
go away, but it can ease us towards
a better frame of mind in which
to meet them. What's on offer is
perspective. Tomorrow will be hard,
but it's one day among many. We're
going to confront a painful side of our
lives, but it's not the only side. It will
be hard, but only comparatively so.
There's still much that is basically OK.

We are small and vast, complicated and simple, deeply odd and unique and yet not so unlike many other people. Tomorrow will come and we will cope.

Lemon and ginger tea

Ingredients:
1 lemon, sliced
2 tbsp fresh ginger, peeled and thinly
sliced
honey, to serve

Prep and cook time: 10 minutes
Makes: 4 servings

1   Place the lemon slices and ginger in a saucepan. Add 1 litre water.

2   Bring to the boil over a high heat.

3   Remove from the heat and let steep for 5 minutes.

4   Strain into serving cups or mugs and sweeten to taste with honey
before serving.

Warm the pot, choose a nice cup, find a teaspoon, even if you don't actually need one. Listen to the sound of the spoon against the cup as you stir; watch the tiny drama of eddies and whirls.

Jean-Baptiste-Siméon Chardin, *Woman Taking Tea*, 1735.

Like the lady in Chardin's painting from 1735, we're narrowing our focus. We're absorbed in the cup, the spoon, the hint of steam rising from the hot liquid; our attention is absorbed by the savour of the tea. At the same time, we're expanding our horizons. We're creatures of many years and many moods; the cosmos is vast and we are tiny, insignificant particles; we used to care about things that mean nothing to us now; we have little idea how our lives will be in five or ten years' time; across the globe few people know us or care about out triumphs or failures; we are the strangest beings we can imagine, capable of thinking about ourselves, capable of imagining things that can never happen. We are small and vast, complicated and simple, odd and unique and yet not so unlike many other people. Tomorrow will come and we will cope.

Pickled herring smørrebrød

Ingredients:

4 asparagus spears, woody
ends removed
4 rye bread slices
2 tbsp butter, softened
200 g | 7 oz pickled herring fillets,
drained, see Tips
4 tbsp crème fraîche
1 tbsp seeds such as pumpkin
or sunflower

1 small handful fresh herbs if
available such as chervil,
or tarragon, torn
flaked sea salt
freshly ground black pepper

Prep and cook time: 10 minutes
Makes: 4 servings

1   Cook the asparagus spears in a saucepan of salted, boiling water until just tender to the tip of a knife, about 2–3 minutes. Drain well and refresh in a bowl of iced water.

2   Drain again, pat dry with kitchen paper, and peel into long, thin ribbons with a vegetable peeler.

3   Spread the rye bread slices with butter and top with the pickled herring fillets and asparagus ribbons.

4   Top with dollops of crème fraîche and scatter the seeds and herbs on top. Season with flaked sea salt and some pepper.

Tips
Smørrebrød (a traditional Scandinavian open-faced sandwich) is a quick and easy meal of rye bread topped with the contents of your store cupboard or fridge. Tinned fish such as sardines also work well.

Vegetarian smørrebrød

Ingredients:

4 rye bread slices
2 tbsp butter, softened
4 tbsp cream cheese
8 salad radishes, thinly sliced
2 tbsp hard cheese such as Gruyère,
or Comté, grated or shaved
2 tsp lemon zest, finely grated
1 handful dill, torn
flaked sea salt

freshly ground black pepper

Prep and cook time: 10 minutes

Makes: 4 servings

1   Toast the rye bread in a toaster or under a hot grill.

2   Let cool briefly before spreading with the butter and then the cream cheese. Top with the radishes, cheese, lemon zest and dill.

3   Season with a little flaked sea salt and pepper before serving.

Sometimes a hug can be just a perfunctory social routine. It can be over-enthusiastic or even unwelcome, but, at best, it is a profound, wordless gesture of tenderness. It's been a difficult day; the news is bleak; the world seems out of control; we're feeling fragile and uncertain. Another holds not just our body but also our troubles and fears.

A hug does not resolve the problems we face, but it shows us we have a companion who is with us, who understands as much as they can. The physical contact comforts us in ways that words – which speak to our adult brains – cannot quite manage. We feel again a little of what perhaps we felt as a child when a loving adult cradled us in their arms. We are participating, briefly, in the cosmic gesture of sympathy.

Painted around 1500 by Sandro Botticelli, *The Mystical Nativity* includes at the bottom a row of angels each delicately hugging a human being in an act of compassion for the sorrows of ordinary existence. Because we can't wait for divine beings and there isn't always another person to hand who can embrace us, we need certain foods that can

Sandro Botticelli, *The Mystical Nativity* (detail), c. 1500–1.

provide something of what we're looking for.

The aromatic noodle soup laksa combines the umami saltiness of shrimp with the rich creaminess of coconut in a consoling group hug, whilst its chilli kick warms us from within. The crucial physical, bodily generosity is there in the rich, savoury taste, offering us all it can: its kindly presence.

Laksa

Ingredients:

For the paste:

1 tsp ground coriander
1 tsp ground cumin
1 tsp turmeric
2 small onions, roughly chopped
50 ml | 3 tbsp coconut milk
3 cm | 1" piece of galangal, peeled and roughly chopped
2 garlic cloves, roughly chopped
2 stalks lemongrass
2-3 red chillies, seeds removed, roughly chopped
1 tbsp shrimp paste

For the soup:

250 g | 9 oz uncooked de-veined prawns
2 tbsp vegetable oil
350 ml | 1 ½ cups coconut milk
500 ml | 2 cups chicken stock
2 dried kaffir lime leaves
1 tbsp soft brown sugar
3-4 tbsp fish sauce
100 g | 3 ½ oz dried egg noodles
1 large lime, juice only
chilli seasoning (powder or flakes), to taste
Handful of beansprouts
1 large spring onion, sliced
salt, to taste
large handful of coriander leaves, to garnish
1 large lime, sliced into wedges, to garnish

Prep and cook time: 30 minutes
Prep and cook time: 2 servings

1   Put the paste ingredients into a food processor and process to a smooth paste. Alternatively, skip this step and use store bought laksa paste.

2   For the soup, heat vegetable oil in a large wok and cook the laksa paste for a minute until it deepens in colour.

3   Stir in the coconut milk, stock, dried kaffir lime leaves, sugar and fish sauce and 250 ml | 1 cup water.

4   Bring the soup to the boil and simmer for 20 minutes until the flavour deepens.

5   Meanwhile, cook the noodles according to the packet instructions and add to the soup.

6   Add the raw prawns and cook for a further two minutes.

7   Season the soup with lime juice, salt and dried chilli flakes. Add the beansprouts and spring onion.

8   Remove the kaffir lime leaves. Garnish with coriander leaves and lime wedges.

'I wish I lived in the countryside'

To those of us forced to live in the city, the idea of the countryside can seem beguiling. We daydream of coming home in the early evening after a long walk across the fields, leaving the muddy boots by the door, padding about the kitchen in chunky woollen socks, lighting the wood fire and casting a last glance out of the window at the dark fruit trees or the vegetable patch before we close the thick curtains.

It could be lovely – but family, work, the allure of nightlife or the desire to be at the centre of things tie us to the city. There's a touch of sadness to the thought that we'll probably never live in the last house in a small village overlooking a brook (even if we know, deep down, that we might get fed up after a few weeks).

However, as with many longings that might not work out perfectly in reality, we can use food to comfort the parts of ourselves that feel neglected in the life we are actually living.

People who live in the country don't necessarily eat pies and stews every day. They may be drawn to food that speaks more of urbanity and metropolitan sophistication. But it is the idea of life away from the city that we're communing with, not the actuality, and inwardly we enrich ourselves with examples of classic countryside fare.

Root vegetable and barley stew

Ingredients:

2 tbsp olive oil
2 onions, chopped
2 leeks, roughly sliced
½ swede, peeled and chopped
2 large parsnips, peeled and roughly chopped
4 baby carrots, trimmed and halved
200 g | 7 oz | 1 cup pearl barley
175 ml dry white wine
1000 ml | 35 fl oz | 4 cups vegetable stock

2 fresh bay leaves
4 thyme sprigs
2 rosemary sprigs
2 tbsp butter
1 handful flat-leaf parsley, chopped
sea salt
freshly ground black pepper

Prep and cook time: 1 hour 15 minutes
Makes: 4 servings

1   Heat the oil in a casserole dish set over a medium heat until hot.

2   Add the onions, leeks and a generous pinch of salt, sweating until softened, about 10 minutes.

3   Stir in the swede, parsnips and carrots, cooking for a further 5 minutes.

4   Stir in the pearl barley and wine. Bring to the boil and let the wine reduce by about half before covering with the stock. Stir in the bay leaves, thyme and rosemary.

5   Return to the boil, cover with a lid, and cook over a reduced heat until the barley has absorbed the stock and the vegetables are tender, about 45 minutes; stir from time to time.

6   When ready, stir in the butter and some salt and pepper to taste; discard the herbs. Divide between bowls and garnish with some chopped parsley.

'I want to contribute
meaningfully'

One of the most effective ways to feel better is, paradoxically, to do something meaningful for someone else. Every time we manage to ameliorate another's life, our own improves in proportion. It tends to be easier to bring a smile to a friend's face than to our own. We are at points in such a tangle of troubles and misery, it seems wisest to halt on the project of increasing our own satisfaction and to turn to others instead.

We are probably already contributing to other people; they're just not that grateful. If we're a parent and helping our child through adolescence, for instance, we might not get thanked for a decade or more – and a lot of the time we're liable to be the recipients of a stream of grunts and insults. Our contribution almost certainly is real; it just doesn't feel that way. The same may hold at work, where we might be doing a lot that overall helps the business but, especially in a large organisation, our contribution is rarely reflected back to us with gratitude and recognition.

This is where the gift of food comes in. When making food for someone else, we get to see smiles and hear words of praise and thanks. We can witness the effect that we are having on another. Giving a friend a jar of homemade jam isn't going to change their existence. But it's tempting always to see 'making a difference' in grand terms, involving sweeping political change and the solution to all the pressing geopolitical problems. These things mostly lie far outside our capacity to achieve much. However, we do have the power to effect change on those closer to home. This may seem small-scale, but it has a large implication. So much of the suffering of the world is intimate: it has to do with loneliness, anxiety and self-doubt. In giving someone a small, sincere gift we've made ourselves, we are – almost without knowing it – targeting one of the most solemn priorities of the human race.

A batch of gooseberry jam

Ingredients:
900 g | 6 cups gooseberries, stems
and dried ends removed
75 ml water
450 g | 2 cups caster sugar
1 tsp butter (optional)

Prep and cook time: 1 hour 10 minutes
Makes: 2 × 450 g jars

1   Combine the gooseberries and water in a large, high-sided saucepan.
Stir well and bring the mixture to the boil over a high heat, crushing the
berries very slightly with a wooden spoon if they do not break down naturally.

2   Once boiling, add the sugar and stir gently until dissolved. If desired, add
the butter to the saucepan at this point.

3   Return the jam to a boil and then reduce the heat to medium and boil until
thickened and the temperature registers 103–104°C | 217–219F on a sugar or
jam thermometer, 20–30 minutes.

4   Ladle the jam into sterilised jam jars, leaving 1 cm | ½" headspace,
and wipe the rims. Add warm lids and rings and seal well.

5   Process the jars in a large saucepan of boiling water for 10 minutes. Turn
off the heat and allow to cool in the saucepan for 5 minutes and then remove.
Leave to cool and then store in a cool, dark place or in the fridge.

Tips
To sterilise jars, wash them in hot, soapy water or put through the hot cycle of
a dishwasher. Do not dry off – instead, place the wet jars into an oven set to
160°C (140° fan) | 325F | gas 3 for 15 minutes. Leave to cool before filling.

'I wish it was still summer'

We try to control our environment in many ways, but never manage to do so entirely. The weather and the seasons continue to exert an enormous influence on our moods. We can be dragged into sadness by the bare branches of the trees, the darker mornings and earlier dusks and the damp, grey afternoons. It's odd to feel how dependent our mood can be on the gyrations of the planet and the long, seasonal tilting away of our place on the earth from the rays of the sun. It's a humbling reminder of our animal nature – the degree to which we are designed to be creatures of the open air and the warm sunlight. On dark days, we may think fondly back to the best of summer: shimmering, inviting mornings, warm evenings, the afternoon sunlight filtering through the full leaves of the trees in the park, the light clothes, the open windows, the pleasure of a shady spot on a hot, cloudless day.

But even when all this is gone, there are foods that can sum up for us the essence of summer and – as it were – bottle the season for us; making a fresher, lighter mood more available to us in the gloom.

We're not just tasting something nice; it's as if we're reconnecting with our summer selves. Taste and smell have the power to reawaken dormant parts of our personality. They summon back to life the freer, easier person we were (and will be once again) in the bright warmth of next year's midsummer.

Lemonade

Ingredients:
3 lemons
75 g | ⅓ cup sugar
500 ml water
soda water, to serve
lemon slices, to serve

Prep and cook time: 30 minutes
Steeping time: 24 hours
Makes: 4 servings

1   Juice the lemons, reserving the skins, and place the juice in a pan with the sugar and water.

2   Bring to a boil, stirring from time time time, then remove the pan from the heat and add the skins.

3   Let the mixture steep for 24 hours then strain through a sieve.

4   Serve the lemonade in glasses filled with ice, top up with soda water and add the lemon slices.

'I need a kickstart'

For all kinds of reasons, we may
hit a sluggish patch in our day.
We were up too late last night; we've
been focusing too long on a fiddly
task; too many demands seem to be
coming our way and we're starting
to buckle; the mind keeps straying.
We know in principle that we can
manage, but the brain won't shift into
a higher gear.

There are plenty of things that might
help: a short nap, a brisk walk, a quick
shower or a chat with an energetic
friend. But also, and significantly,
taking a few minutes to make (and
eat) a piquant meal can give us just
the right mixture of a short break,
a purposeful distraction, and a jolt
of stimulation, so we can go back
refreshed and more buoyant to all
the arduous things we still have
to do.

Pan-seared tuna

Ingredients:
200g | 7 oz tuna steak, approx. 3cm thick
125g | 5 oz small new potatoes,

For the sauce:
1 small clove of garlic, peeled
1 tbsp fresh parsley, leaves only
1 tbsp fresh basil, leaves only
½ tbsp capers

½ tbsp gherkins
½ tbsp anchovies, rinsed if packed in salt
1 tsp Dijon mustard
1 tsp red wine vinegar
2 tbsp extra-virgin olive oil

Prep time: 10 minutes
Cook time: 10 minutes
Makes: 1 serving

1   For the sauce, finely chop the garlic, herbs, capers, gherkins and anchovies. Alternatively, pulse the ingredients in a food processor. Transfer to a bowl and add the mustard and vinegar. Slowly add the olive oil until you reach the desired consistency. Season to taste with salt and pepper and set aside.

2   Cook the new potatoes in lightly salted boiling water for 6–8 minutes, or until tender. Drain, toss with the butter and season with salt and pepper.

3   Meanwhile, rub a little oil onto each side of the tuna steak and season with salt and pepper. Heat a griddle and sear briefly for 2 minutes on each side

4   Serve the tuna steak with potatoes, steamed green beans and a generous helping of the sauce.

'I need to get away'

The feeling of being at home answers to a profound need; but it's understandable that we can have too much of this good thing. Where we are now, even if it's a good place, may not speak to all of who we are, and who we might be. There are always potential selves waiting for the right stimulus, some of which might have to come from somewhere else. It's what we experience in the better moments of travel, when we feel expanded and even transformed by our discovery of a new place.

We get fed up not because what is familiar is horrible, but because we're longing to meet the interesting parts of ourselves that come to the fore in places that are, to us, exotic. They're exotic not simply because they are new and strange, but because a part of us is more at home there than in the place where we usually live. Another culture, a different way of living, another perspective on the priorities of existence, appeals because it chimes with a sense of our true identity: this foreign aspect is who we are as well. Logically, we could have been born anywhere; we might have grown up with a very different set of values and interests – and we'd still be us, just in a different guise.

Food can help us locate and hold on to the foreign parts of who we are. The combination of spice, sweetness and savouriness may be unfamiliar, but as we eat we can imagine another life for ourselves in which this would have been familiar from childhood onwards.

As the food we prepare understands, an important part of us always belongs elsewhere.

Punjabi style beetroot

Ingredients:

2 large beetroot, scrubbed and trimmed
1 tbsp sunflower oil
1 lemon, juiced
1 small red onion, finely diced
1 tbsp fresh ginger, peeled and finely chopped
1 green chilli, seeded and finely chopped

1 tsp amchoor, dried mango powder
1 small handful coriander, chopped
salt
freshly ground black pepper

Prep and cook time: 1 hour 10 minutes
Chilling time: 30 minutes
Makes: 4 servings

1   Preheat the oven to 180°C (160° fan) | 350F | gas 4.

2   Rub the beetroot with the oil and wrap in aluminium foil. Place on a rimmed baking tray and bake until tender to the tip of a knife, about 1 hour.

3   Remove from the oven and let cool on the tray.

4   Once cool enough to handle, peel and dice the beetroot. Transfer to a mixing bowl and add the lemon juice, red onion, ginger, chilli, amchoor, and plenty of salt and pepper to taste.

5   Cover and chill for 30 minutes.

6   When ready to serve, remove from the fridge and garnish with coriander.

'I need an early night'

To a surprising, and almost humiliating extent, some of the gravest problems we face during a day can be traced back to a brutally simple fact: we did not sleep enough the night before.

The idea sounds offensive. There are surely greater issues than tiredness. We are likely to be up against genuine hurdles: the economic situation, politics, problems at work, tensions in our relationship, the family … These are true difficulties. But what we often fail to appreciate is the extent to which our ability to confront them with courage and resilience is dependent on a range of distinctly 'small' or 'low' factors: what our blood sugar level is like, when we last had proper reassurance from someone, how much water we've drunk – and how many hours we've rested.

We tend to resist such analyses of our troubles. It can feel like an insult to our rational, adult dignity to think that our sense of gloom might in the end stem from exhaustion. We'd sooner identify ourselves as up against an existential crisis than see ourselves as sleep-deprived.

Yet we should be careful of under- but also of over-intellectualising. To be happy, we require large, serious things (money, freedom, love), and a lot of semi-insultingly little things too (a good diet, hugs, rest).

Anyone who has ever looked after babies knows this well. When life becomes too much for them, it is almost always because they are tired, thirsty or hungry. With this in mind, it should be no insult to insist that we never allow ourselves to adopt a tragic stance until we have first made ourselves a simple, easily digestible meal at around 7 p.m. and fallen asleep by 9 p.m.

Miso and chicken noodle soup

Ingredients:

150 g | 5 oz chicken, skinless and boneless

3 tbsp miso paste

1 tsp tomato paste

1 tsp fresh ginger, peeled and sliced

1 clove garlic

3–4 mushrooms, thinly sliced

2 tbsp sweetcorn

50 g | 2 oz rice noodles

Small bunch fresh coriander leaves

2 spring onions, sliced into rings

1 red chilli pepper, deseeded and chopped

Prep and cook time: 30 minutes

Makes: 2 servings

1   Put the chicken in a pot with 900 ml | 4 cups cold water. Add the miso and tomato paste, peppercorns, salt, ginger and garlic. Bring to a boil over high heat then turn down to a simmer and cook for approximately 20 minutes until the chicken is done.

2   Remove the chicken from the pot and shred into bite-sized pieces.

3   Return to the pot with the vegetable and noodles. Simmer for 5 minutes until noodles are cooked.

4   Put the meat and noodles into 4 bowls and top with the spring onions and chopped chillies. Pour over the hot broth and garnish with the chopped coriander.

There may be many causes of insomnia, from drinking too much coffee to a sinus infection. But there's one important factor that's not often given enough attention: what's going on in our minds. Insomnia should frequently be understood as the revenge of the thoughts we didn't take seriously enough in the day. We're in bed at 3 a.m. and there's a swirling mess in our minds: odd strands of memory, feelings of regret, anxiety about what's facing us in the morning. We lie awake worrying because we didn't give these issues the attention they needed earlier.

Therefore, a good response to insomnia is to help ourselves think and sort out what's on or minds before we go to bed. We might not typically use the name, but what we're looking for is a bit of timely philosophical meditation before we retire. This is the routine of clarifying what's on our minds by asking (and trying to answer) three key questions:

What am I presently anxious about?
What am I presently upset about?
What am I presently excited about?

The role of food before bed might not be so much to settle our stomachs or create a pleasant feeling of drowsiness; instead what we want is to give ourselves a quiet, focused period in which we can think things through. We suggest something that takes 30 minutes to simmer, giving you a vital window of time to jot down your thoughts and clear your head before bedtime.

Tomato soup

Ingredients:

25 g | 2 tbsp unsalted butter
1 small white onion, cut into quarters
1 tin (400 g | 14 oz) plum tomatoes,
roughly mashed
Salt and pepper to taste

Prep time: 2 minutes
Cook time: 30 minutes
Makes: 1 generous serving

1   Place butter, onion and tinned tomatoes in a small pan over a medium heat and bring to a gentle simmer.

2   Cook uncovered for about 30 minutes.

3   Once the onion is completely cooked and soft, blend the soup in a food processor or blender with a little water until smooth and creamy.

Looking after ourselves

3
With friends

With friends

One of the major obstacles to developing a good social life is the idea that doing so might be easy. Living well around other people, deepening and nourishing friendships, learning how to speak to someone with directness and vulnerability, hearing someone else's story without interrupting or shutting them down are all part of an art that we are too seldom taught and rarely even think we might have to learn.

We accept that we will have to acquire skills to cook, but food can only ever be as fulfilling as the conversation and friendship that unfolds around it.

In an ideal world, we wouldn't divide the two tasks: learning how to cook would mean, more broadly, learning how to nourish – in mind and spirit – those we love.

'A whole group are coming round:
it felt like a great idea when I
asked them, now I'm panicking...'

The panic isn't really about the practicalities of getting everything organised before the doorbell rings. It has a deeper root: we are unsure whether we can live up to the expectations we have raised in others. In inviting our friends, we haven't only offered them a meal, we have put ourselves forward as the choreographers of their happiness for a few hours.

Now we are daunted and unsure. We rack our brains for ideas of what might please. We saw a recipe involving papaya, soy beans and chicken; someone mentioned a wonderful dish involving goat's cheese and marinated liver they'd had in Spain; we hastily flick through a beautifully illustrated book of Middle Eastern recipes we've never yet explored.

We seek inspiration from evidence of what other, more prestigious human beings have liked. In our distress, we forget to tap into the most powerful resource we have: our existing knowledge of what gives us pleasure. In our distress, the last person we think of consulting is ourselves. We discard the claims of dishes we've reliably enjoyed for years,

that we liked when we were twelve and still like now when we're on our own. There's a curious, misdirected modesty that can cause us to assume that others will be too sophisticated or too worldly to be charmed or delighted by something that is endorsed by nothing more than our own humble experience.

Curiously, the most satisfying moments in the history of art often involve independent-minded people learning to take their own pleasures seriously, and then discovering that many others are charmed by them too.

In the 18th century, when most artists were painting grand scenes of aristocratic life or pivotal moments in the Gospel stories, the Welsh artist Thomas Jones stayed loyal to the pleasure he found in small-scale sights of ordinary existence: in washing hung out to dry, for example, or old stone walls. He wasn't trying to second-guess what might be attractive to others; he was following the sources of his own pleasure. In the process, Jones turned out some of the most delightful pictures ever made.

Thomas Jones, *A Wall in Naples*, 1782.

Jones's art grew out of the same question that lies behind good entertaining: 'what, honestly, do I like?' Not: 'what might impress the world?' but 'what have I found that works for me?'

It is a tricky question to answer honestly when guests on whose affections we depend will be here in a few hours. Our tastes won't be exactly the same as everyone else's, but we stand a higher chance of fulfilling other people when we stay true to that vital source of data: our own appetite.

Coq au vin

Ingredients:

4 tbsp butter
8 shallots, quartered
75 g | 2 ½ oz | ½ cup bacon
3 cloves garlic, chopped
1 bunch small carrots, peeled with tops trimmed
1 bunch baby turnips, peeled and quartered
1 chicken; ~1.4 kg, jointed
200 ml | 7 fl oz | ⅞ cup chicken stock
300 ml | 11 fl oz | 1 ⅓ cups red wine
3 fresh bay leaves

1 handful fresh thyme sprigs
4 juniper berries
1 tsp black peppercorns
200 g | 7 oz | 2 ½ cups small mushrooms, cleaned with stems removed
1 handful flat-leaf parsley, chopped
sea salt
freshly ground black pepper

Prep and cook time: 1 hour 15 minutes
Makes: 4 servings

1   Preheat the oven to 180°C (160° fan) | 350F | gas 4.

2   Heat 2 tablespoons butter in a roasting dish and fry the shallots, bacon, garlic, carrots and turnips for 6–8 minutes.

3   Deglaze with the stock and red wine, then add the bay leaves, thyme, juniper berries and peppercorns. Season with salt.

4   Arrange the chicken pieces in the roasting dish. Cover the dish with aluminium foil and bake in the oven for 35 minutes.

5   Melt the remaining butter in a pan and fry the mushrooms with a generous pinch of salt until lightly browned. Add the mushrooms and parsley to the roasting dish. Return to the oven uncovered, cooking until the chicken is cooked through, about 10–15 minutes.

6   Remove from the oven and let stand briefly before serving. The gratin recipe on the next page serves as a vegetarian option, or a hearty accompaniment to the chicken.

Potato and vegetable gratin

Ingredients:

600 g | 21 oz | 4 cups potatoes, peeled and sliced

2 medium sweet potatoes, peeled and sliced

400 g | 14 oz | 2 ⅔ cups pumpkin, sliced

sea salt and pepper

300 ml | 11 fl oz | 1 ⅓ cups soured cream

100 ml | 3 ½ fl oz | 7 tbsp vegetable stock

1 tbsp grain mustard

1 free-range egg, beaten

200 g | 7 oz | 1 cup mozzarella cheese, thinly sliced

200 g | 7 oz | 2 cups Cheddar, grated

1 tbsp chopped fresh thyme, plus extra sprigs to garnish

Prep and cook time: 1 hour

Makes: 4 servings

1   Preheat the oven to 200°C (180° fan) | 400F | gas 6. Butter a large baking dish.

2   Put the potatoes in a pan and cover with water. Add a pinch of salt and bring to a boil. Cook for 5 minutes. Add the sweet potatoes and pumpkin and cook for a further 3 minutes. Drain well and set aside.

3   Mix together the soured cream, stock, mustard and egg in a mixing bowl. Season with salt and pepper.

4   Layer the potatoes, sweet potatoes, pumpkin and mozzarella in the baking dish, sprinkling each layer with grated cheese and thyme, finishing with a layer of potatoes. Pour over the soured cream mixture, brushing it over the top layer of potatoes.

5   Cover with foil and cook for 30 minutes. Remove the foil and continue cooking for a further 15–20 minutes until the potatoes are tender and browned. Sprinkle with thyme and serve.

'My extended family is coming round: What on earth do I have in common with them?'

Our Romantic conception of social life focuses on getting together with people who have much in common with us: we're searching for soul mates – or at least people who share our interests and outlook.

But when we entertain, a lot of our time will be spent hosting that far more fractious and awkward proposition: our extended families, people we didn't choose as friends and might disagree with about many things, but who we will have to keep living around because clan loyalty demands it.

The core thing about families is that we're related to people we might never have chosen. There's an uncle whose political views are totally opposed to our own; we've a young cousin who is passionately into ice-skating or a TV show we've never heard of; we've maybe acquired a glamorous stepmother as a consequence of our father's mid-life adventures.

It feels as though chance has set us down in the middle of a group of aliens. We're maybe going to be spending a few hours in the company of a brother-in-law who is involved in the accountancy problems of middle-sized businesses or Icelandic archaeology, topics that we'd reflexively regard as of no interest whatever.

But in a more Classical view of social life, we honour the role these people play for us. They provide the opportunity for a degree of intimacy with types whom our own native inclinations would never prompt us to get to know. We can hear, at first hand, why someone honestly ends up with views we find outlandish, which is a valuable (but rarely accessed) source of information; we can learn to see the grace and excitement of activities we'd instinctively consider unworthy of our notice; we may get to hear the inside story, the secret tribulations, and the special pleasures of people we'd otherwise feel intimidated by or dismissive of.

It's the sheer oddity of our family members that, paradoxically, is their greatest advantage. Our natural wish may be to run away. But if we stick with the task, we'll be receiving an education in the wider reality of the lives and loves of others that corrects the stubborn, invisible biases of our own ideas and preferences.

A whole chicken is oddly apt for a
family meal: unlike most dishes, its
distinct parts please different people;
the dark, gelatinous thigh, the leg
that invites us to eat with our hands;
the delicate wing, the mild flesh of the
breast, the small succulent pockets of
meat hidden on the underside.

Ask someone to carve, invite others
to start passing round the gravy
and the vegetables. When the chicken
is pretty much finished, get the oldest
and youngest to pull the wishbone
(the Y-shaped bone at the top of
the neck) and each make a wish,
which they should be prepared to
share aloud.

Roast chicken

Ingredients:

2 large chickens – approx. 2kg | 4 ½ lbs each, giblets removed, see Tips

2 unwaxed lemons, quartered

2 large onions, quartered

handful of rosemary

6 bay leaves

4 whole garlic heads, cut across the middle

3 kg potato, peeled and quartered

4 tbsp mild olive oil

100 g butter, softened

Prep and cook time: 2 hours

Rest time: 10 minutes

Makes: 10–12 servings

1   Preheat the oven to 190°C (170° fan) | 375F | gas 5.

2   Season chicken cavities with salt and pepper. Fill each cavity with lemons, onion, rosemary, bay leaves and half of the garlic. Tie legs together with twine.

3   Toss potatoes and remaining garlic in oil and season with salt and pepper.

4   Arrange chickens on the roasting tin side by side and place potato and garlic around the edges. Make sure they are evenly spaced in the tin. Brush chickens generously with butter and season with salt and pepper. Roast for approximately 1 hour 40 minutes checking to baste with butter 2–3 times.

5   Remove chickens and cover loosely with tin foil to rest.

6   Turn the oven up to 230°C | (210° fan) | 450F | gas 7 and return potatoes and garlic to crisp up for an additional 10–15 minutes whilst meat is resting. Serve with steamed green vegetables and gravy.

Tips

To calculate cooking time, use the following calculation: 20 minutes per 500g | 1 lb + 20 minutes. Only account for the weight of a single bird.

Spinach and nut loaf

Ingredients:

150 g | 5 oz | 6 cups baby spinach
130 g | 4 ½ oz | 1 cup cashews
250 g | 9 oz | 2 cups hazelnuts
300 g | 11 oz | 2 cups cooked
chestnuts, chopped
2 small onions, finely chopped
2 celery stalks, finely chopped
1 small carrot, diced
2 cloves garlic, minced
75 ml | 2 ½ fl oz | ⅓ cup sunflower oil
2 large free-range eggs, beaten

40 g | 1 ½ oz | ⅓ cup cornflour
125 g | 4 ½ oz | 1 cup plain flour
½ tsp baking powder
salt
freshly ground black pepper

Prep and cook time: 1 hour 20 minutes

Makes: 4 servings

1   Preheat the oven to 180°C (160° fan) | 350F | gas 4. Grease and line a
900 g | 2 lb loaf tin with greaseproof paper.

2   Steam the spinach in a steaming basket set over a saucepan of simmering
water, about 3 minutes. Drain and use kitchen paper to soak up any excess
water before chopping.

3   Combine the cashews, hazelnuts, chestnuts, onions, celery, carrot, garlic
and seasoning in a food processor. Pulse until finely chopped. Put in a bowl
with the oil, eggs, cornflour, flour, baking powder. Mix thoroughly. Add the
spinach before transferring the mixture into the prepared loaf tin.

4   Rap the tin a few times on a work surface. Cover the tin with aluminium
foil. Bake for 20 minutes then remove the foil. Bake for another 25–30 minutes
until golden on top, slightly risen and dry to the touch. When ready, a cake
tester should come out clean from its centre.

5   Remove to a wire rack to cool slightly before turning out, slicing and
serving.

'Some kids are coming round and they swear they will never eat a vegetable'

It's a familiar complaint from children: vegetables are boring – and we might have felt the same when we were their age. The problem is that we know that vegetables are good for us, and we want our children to have a healthy diet. However, we don't want to be aligned with the miserable cultural image of the stern, old-fashioned parent who grimly serves up boiled cabbage and soggy Brussels sprouts: they taste awful and there'll be a row.

The attempt to get a child to eat a balanced diet is an instance of a huge, almost eternal problem of human culture: how to encourage others to do things they really should do, but that don't much appeal. Typically, we turn to nagging and sanctions to wear down or overcome resistance. It's an exhausting approach and it doesn't work.

A better strategy was developed in an unexpected place: Renaissance art. In 15th-century Italy, Catholic religious leaders wanted people to go to their churches, but instead of threatening or insisting they turned to what is properly called seduction. They commissioned architects to design enchanting buildings, they employed composers to produce thrilling music, they hired artists to paint pictures of alluring male and female saints. The goal was still to get people to do some uncomfortable things: to consider their sins, to repent, to be more charitable and to spend a portion of every Sunday listening to a sermon. However, by appealing to the senses and the emotions, they made these useful but unappealing things more palatable.

The Renaissance approach to children and diet focuses on making good things as charming and inviting as possible. It means not fighting their preferences but cleverly incorporating healthy ingredients into dishes that probably appeal already.

Beetroot brownies

Ingredients:
300g | 10 oz cooked beetroot
100 g | ½ cup unsalted butter,
plus extra for greasing the tin
200g | 1 ¼ cups dark chocolate,
roughly chopped
1 tsp vanilla extract
250g | 1 ⅓ cups golden caster sugar
3 eggs
100g | ⅞ cup plain flour
25g | 2 tbsp cocoa powder

Prep time: 5 minutes
Cook time: 40 minutes
Makes: 16 brownies

1   Preheat oven to 180°C (160° fan) | 350F | gas 4. Butter and line a baking tin – approximately 25 × 25 cm | 10 × 10".

2   Place cooked beetroot into a food processor and blend until you have a smooth puree.

3   Place chocolate and butter over a low heat and melt. Combine with the pureed beetroot and add the vanilla extract. Set to one side.

4   Beat the sugar and eggs together until pale and thick (about 2 minutes).

5   Using a metal spoon, gently fold the beetroot mixture into the bowl.

6   Sift in the flour and cocoa powder, again gently folding in to conserve the air in the mixture.

7   Pour into the tin and bake for 25–30 minutes until just cooked. Leave to cool in the tin and then cut into squares.

'I'm cooking for some intimidating people and don't know how to charm them'

Typically, we suppose that it is our most impressive sides that will appeal to others. That's why we aim to be flawless and perfect over lunch or dinner, as much in our anecdotes as in our dishes.

We tend to steer people's attention towards our successes and present them with impressive menus. We want them to like us, so we let them know how happy we are in our new job, how pleased we are with the way the garden is coming on, how we've just booked a holiday – and how skilled we are at making Shanghai soup dumplings or Mocha Dacquoise.

However, what actually endears us to other people is the revelation of our failings and vulnerabilities – the ways we've messed up and made mistakes. The admission of vulnerability is a key route to intimacy; it allows the other person to admit that they too are not always impressive, quite often scared, and full of regrets. Perfection can impress and intimidate, but it is our flaws that ultimately build friendships.

In this spirit, it's worth getting ambitious about a meal, but in the knowledge that a complicated dish might not come off and it might

even be a good thing if it doesn't. A lopsided or discoloured creation introduces to the table the key ingredients of charm: the frank admission of anxiety; the readiness to admit to our failures, and a distinct grace in presenting our pretensions and ambitions in a comedic vein.

Crab and Gruyère soufflé

Ingredients:

1 dressed crab, brown and white meat

2 tbsp Parmesan cheese, grated

25 g | 2 tbsp butter, for greasing

25 g | 2 tbsp flour

285 ml | 1 ¼ cups milk

½ tsp mustard powder

dash of Tabasco sauce

110 g | 1 cup Gruyère cheese, grated

4 free-range eggs, separated

sea salt and freshly ground black pepper

Prep time: 15 minutes

Cook time: 20 minutes

Makes: 6 servings

1   Preheat the oven to 180°C (160° fan) | 350F | gas 4.

2   Butter the insides of six ramekins and coat with the Parmesan cheese. Shake out any excess.

3   Melt the butter in a saucepan over a medium heat. Stir in the flour and mustard. Cook for a minute. Take off the heat and gradually whisk in the milk.

4   Return to the heat and gently cook the sauce until thickened. Add the Tabasco, Gruyère and seasoning, mixing until fully incorporated. Gently stir in the crab meat.

5   Transfer the mixture to a bowl and allow to cool. Beat in the egg yolks.

6   In a separate bowl whisk the egg whites until peaks form that just hold their shape. Add the egg whites to the crab mixture and gently fold in using a metal spoon. Spoon the mixture evenly into the six ramekins. To encourage an even rise run a cutlery knife around the inner edge of each ramekin.

7   Cook in the oven for 20 minutes or until risen and golden.

8   Serve at once. Try not to worry if they collapse.

'How can I be a 'warm' host?'

There is a kind of host who follows every rule of etiquette and outward sign of civility, yet who may still come across as coldly polite, leaving their guests a little bored and with no urgent wish to return for more.

Being warm means remembering that the priority in social life isn't extreme rule-bound politeness: it's humanity. Politeness has many merits, but there's a moment at which it starts to separate us from others. To put people at their ease when we want to build a friendship, we have to show our more normal, day-to-day and less elevated sides. We should reveal that we have basic needs and earthy desires. Warmth comes from being upfront about these tendencies in ourselves and recognising them in others.

Finger foods like tacos at once humanise the table: it's impossible to be too precious, and that is the fun of it. Hold the soft tortilla in your hands and try not to let the filling fall out and invite guests to do likewise; it's tasty and bit messy and sauce gets on our chins and on the table. And no one minds at all.

Fish tacos with coleslaw

Ingredients:

For the coleslaw:

2 tbsp mayonnaise
1 tbsp crème fraîche
1 tsp mustard powder
2 tbsp white wine vinegar
450 g | 1lb oz | 3 cups cabbage, finely sliced
1 carrot, peeled and finely sliced

For the tacos:

600 g | 21 oz | 4 cups white fish, e.g. cod, skinned, diced and pin-boned
1 lime, juiced
plain flour, for dusting
4 tbsp sunflower oil
8 individual corn tortillas

Prep and cook time: 45 minutes

Makes: 4 servings

1　Mix together the mayonnaise, crème fraîche, mustard powder and vinegar in a mixing bowl.

2　Season with salt and a pinch of sugar and stir in the remaining coleslaw ingredients. Leave to stand at room temperature for around 15 minutes.

3　Season the fish with salt, pepper and a drizzle of lime juice. Dust with some flour, shaking off the excess.

4　Heat the oil in a large sauté pan until hot. Add the fish and dry on all sides until golden-brown and opaque in appearance, about 3–5 minutes.

5　Serve the fish with the coleslaw and the tacos.

Fried avocado tacos

Ingredients:
2 large eggs
100 g | 3 ½ oz | ¾ cup plain flour
180 g | 6 oz | 2 cups panko breadcrumbs
2 avocados
1000 ml | 35 fl oz | 4 cups vegetable oil, for deep-frying
8 mini flour tortillas
½ iceberg lettuce, shredded

100 g | 3 ½ oz | 1 cup Cheddar
120 g | 4 oz | ½ cup soured cream
1 handful coriander, torn
1 lime, cut into wedges
hot sauce, e.g. Tabasco
sea salt
freshly ground black pepper

Prep and cook time: 30 minutes
Makes: 4 servings

1   Place the eggs, flour and breadcrumbs in three separate shallow dishes or bowls. Season each with salt and pepper and thoroughly beat the eggs with a fork.

2   Halve, pit, peel and cut the avocados into 16 wedges in total. Add to the flour, tossing to coat. Transfer to the egg, turning to coat. Let the excess drip off before transferring to the breadcrumbs, gently pressing the avocado to coat.

3   Heat the oil in a large heavy-based saucepan to 180°C | 356F. Working in two batches, deep-fry the avocado until golden-brown and crisp, about 3 minutes, turning the wedges over in the oil with tongs.

4   When ready, remove from the oil and drain on a plate lined with kitchen paper. Loosely cover with aluminium foil to keep warm as you cook the remaining batch.

5   When ready to serve, warm the tortillas in a dry frying pan set over a medium heat until hot.

6   Fill the tortillas with lettuce, fried avocado, grated Cheddar, soured cream, and coriander. Serve with hot sauce and lime wedges on the side.

Churros with chocolate orange sauce

Ingredients:

200 g | 7 oz | 1 ⅓ cups dark cooking chocolate, chopped
200 ml | 7 fl oz | ⅞ cup double cream
1 tsp orange zest, from an unwaxed orange
300 g | 11 oz | 2 ¾ cups plain flour
vegetable oil, for deep frying
sugar, for dusting

Prep and cook time: 45 minutes

Makes: 15–20 churros

1   Put the chocolate in a metal bowl with the cream and melt, stirring, over a pan of hot water. Allow to cool slightly, then stir in the orange zest.

2   For the dough, bring 500 ml | 2 cups water to the boil with a pinch of salt. Add the flour all in one go and stir with a wooden spoon. Heat, stirring, for 3 minutes until the dough has formed a ball which comes away from the base of the pan. Transfer to a bowl, cover and leave to rest for 10 minutes.

3   Spoon the dough into a piping bag with a medium-sized star nozzle (approximately 1 cm | ½").

4   Heat the oil in a deep saucepan (or deep fat fryer) to approximately 170°C | 340F; the oil is hot enough if small bubbles form around the handle of a wooden spoon.

5   Pipe the dough into the oil in lengths of roughly 12 cm | 4.5", cutting it off at the nozzle with a small knife. Deep-fry the dough for 4–5 minutes until golden brown, turning once. Use a slotted spoon to carefully lift the churros out of the fat, and drain on kitchen paper.

6   Sprinkle with sugar and serve, ideally still warm, with the chocolate sauce for dipping.

Being warm means remembering that the priority in social life isn't extreme rule-bound politeness:
it's humanity.

'How can I be an open-minded host?'

An open-minded host is always ready with the thought that their guests might have things to get off their chests that are contrary to what one might expect given who they seem to be.

The ancient Roman comedy playwright Terence, who lived in the 2nd century BCE, defined the core of open-mindedness: *I am human: nothing human is foreign to me.*

The open-minded person is unsurprised by the oddity of others because they have already recognised a high degree of oddity in themselves. They don't draw conclusions about a person's inner life from externals. They are receptive to who another person might really be: a dishevelled individual might be competent; a neatly attired lawyer might have a raucous sex life; someone who clears up the mess in other people's gardens for a living might be well informed about tax legislation or be a fine tennis player; an eloquent individual might suffer from anxiety attacks; someone who drinks a bit too much might generally be serious and thoughtful. Oddly, we become more open-minded not so much by studying other people but by taking note of the case closest to home: our own. We know that our own inner life has many strange recesses: we might have dark thoughts of violent revenge, even though we'd never carry them out; we might have elaborate fantasies, although we strike others as straight-laced; we're obsessed with money, even though we're committed to the ideal that money shouldn't be a major value; we come across as fairly calm, but we know our own times of rage and despair. The open-minded person keeps their knowledge of themselves at the front of their minds and uses it to imagine what others might be like. They pay the rest of the world a strange compliment: that of assuming that everyone is just as complicated behind the scenes as they are themselves.

Open-mindedness finds its natural place around a welcoming table. With a few friends, we can create an environment where we are able to reveal our odder sides, without fear of judgement or moralism. The process can unfold particularly well around some of the stranger-looking denizens of the sea.

I am human: nothing human is foreign to me.

Terence

Shucked oysters

Ingredients:
80 ml | 3 fl oz | ⅓ cup white wine vinegar
80 ml | 3 fl oz | ⅓ cup red wine vinegar
½ tsp salt
½ tsp freshly ground black pepper
1 pinch caster sugar
2 shallots, finely chopped
16 fresh oysters, with shells

Prep and cook time: 45 minutes
Makes: 4 servings

1   Whisk together the vinegars, salt, pepper and sugar in a small bowl until the sugar and salt have dissolved. Stir in the chopped shallots and set aside for 30 minutes.

2   Scrub the oysters clean under cool running water.

3   Carefully shuck the oysters with a shucking knife; hold the oyster wrapped in a tea towel in one hand and slide the tip of the knife into the hinge of the oyster, located at the thin end where the top and bottom shell meet. Once the tip of the knife is in the oyster, wiggle the knife back along the length of the shell to sever the adductor muscle that is attached to the top shell, opening up the oyster. Try to preserve as much of the oyster liquor as possible.

4   Place the oysters on a bed of crushed ice and serve immediately with the dressing on the side.

Mussels with cider, tarragon and crème fraîche

Ingredients:
1 tbsp unsalted butter
2 large shallots, finely sliced
4 tarragon sprigs, plus extra to serve
1500 g | 53 oz | 10 cups fresh mussel, rinsed with beards removed, see Tips
300 ml | 11 fl oz | 1 ⅓ cups cider, preferably dry
3 tbsp crème fraîche
crusty bread, to serve
freshly ground black pepper

Prep and cook time: 20 minutes
Makes: 4 servings

1   Melt the butter in a large heavy-based saucepan set over a medium heat. Add the shallots and tarragon, sweating until softened, about 3–4 minutes.

2   Increase the heat to high and add the mussels and cider. Cover with a lid and cook until the mussels have steamed opened, shaking the pan from time to time, about 4–6 minutes.

3   Remove the lid and discard any mussels that haven't opened. Transfer the mussels to bowls using a slotted spoon.

4   Return the juices in the pan to a simmer over a moderate heat and stir in the crème fraîche and some pepper to taste.

5   Ladle over the mussels and serve with crusty bread on the side.

Tips
Before cooking, discard any mussels that don't close with a few taps. Remove the beards by firmly pulling on their threads with your fingers.

Fried skate wings with brown butter sauce

Ingredients:
4 skate wings, filleted and skinned
3 tbsp plain flour
4 tbsp unsalted butter
60 ml | 2 fl oz | ¼ cup white wine
sea salt
freshly ground black pepper
2 tbsp chives, finely chopped

Prep and cook time: 20 minutes
Makes: 4 servings

1   Set oven to its lowest temperature and have a baking sheet ready for the skate wings.

2   Rinse and pat the skate wings dry. Season with a little salt. Dredge the skate wings in flour and shake off the excess.

3   Place a pan over a high heat for approximately 3 minutes, once hot, turn down a little and add half the butter to the pan.

4   Add the skate wings to the hot butter and cook for 2–3 minutes each side. Transfer to the baking sheet and place in the warm oven.

5   Put the remaining butter in the pan and cook until light brown. Add the white wine and cook off the alcohol.

6   Serve the skate wings and pour over the brown butter sauce. Garnish with chives. Serve with mashed potatoes.

'Why do we keep talking about house prices and how busy airports are?'

We know our friends are fascinating, but too often, we seem unable to access the valuable parts of them. Maybe we don't get much beyond anecdotes about things that happened at work, what's annoying about the children's schools or the tribulations of the real-estate market. We're used to it, but there's a touch of tragedy about the situation. Each individual is potentially fascinating: they've lived and suffered; they have millions of memories; they've witnessed so much human drama; there are so many ideas and opinions in their minds but only a few fragments make it to the surface in a group conversation.

A remedy lies in an idea that is familiar to us around eating but that we don't currently apply to talking: namely, a menu. In a restaurant, we don't arrive and just think up, off the top of our heads, what we might like to eat. We're given a smallish number of precise suggestions, which we'd probably not have come up with on our own. Seeing them written down jogs our imagination and we realise that they (or some other things on the list) appeal to us.

A conversation menu works in a similar way. It offers a range of prompts, from which we can then make a selection. In the background is the Classical idea that interesting conversation isn't spontaneous; it is the result of preparation and guidance.

Here is a small conversation menu you might try:

First course

•

Describe your character when you were ten.

Main course

•

What's an especially difficult compromise you have made?

Dessert

•

Talk about something you have failed at. How did you react to that failure at the time and how do you feel about it now?

(See p. 353 for more conversation menus.)

We know our friends
are fascinating, but too
often, we seem unable
to access the valuable
parts of them.

'Why the need to be so jolly
all the time?'

Being jolly around the table sounds lovely in theory; but because so much of the human condition is stamped with anguish, dread and remorse, the idea that a good meal invariably has to be a bright and chirpy occasion can get in the way of providing proper hospitality.

Normality includes a lot of sorrows. In the background of most of our lives, there is likely to be a powerful sadness. It's natural to want to skirt contact with it, but such avoidance comes at a high price. Honesty about the darkness inside ourselves and the oddity and cruelty of life more generally are crucial components in achieving intimacy with others.

In a discussion of parenting styles, the pioneering child psychoanalyst Donald Winnicott (1896–1971) once identified a particularly problematic kind of child carer: the person who wants to 'jolly' babies and small children along, picking them up with cheer, bouncing them up and down and pulling exaggeratedly funny faces, perhaps shouting 'peekaboo!' repeatedly. The criticism might feel disconcerting: what could be wrong with wanting to keep a child jolly? Yet Winnicott was worried by what effect this would have on a child – the way it would subtly not give the child a chance to acknowledge its own sadness or, more broadly, its own feelings.

The jollier doesn't just want the child to be happy; more alarmingly, they can't tolerate the idea that the child might be sad, so unexplored and potentially overwhelming are his or her own background feelings of disappointment and grief. Childhood is necessarily full of sadness (as is adulthood), insisted Winnicott, which means we must perpetually be granted the possibility of periods of mourning: for a broken toy, the grey sky on a Sunday afternoon, or the lingering sadness we can see in our parents' eyes.

We need a public culture that remembers how much of life deserves to have solemn and mournful moments and that isn't tempted – normally in the name of selling us things – aggressively to deny the legitimate place of melancholy.

We can use food to encourage the sombre atmosphere we sometimes need. For example, the dark colouring, slightly heavy texture and quiet dignity of a beef or bean stew can invite a more reflective state of mind. It reminds us that our own awareness of the melancholy side of existence isn't some personal quirk. The dish, and all those who have loved it over the centuries and in many places, is on our side. It legitimatises our melancholy, not as an odd thing about us, but as a central, intelligent response to the darker aspects of the human situation.

Beef bourguignon

Ingredients:

900 g | 32 oz | 6 cups braising steak, cut into cubes

3 tbsp oil

450 g | 16 oz | 3 ½ cups shallots, peeled

4 rashers streaky bacon

2 cloves garlic

1 tbsp flour

500 ml | 18 fl oz | 2 cups red Burgundy, or other dry red wine

250 ml | 9 fl oz | 1 cup beef stock

2 large carrots, peeled and cut into chunks

2 sprigs thyme

2 bay leaves

50 g | 1 ¾ oz | ¼ cup butter

200 g | 7 oz | 2 ¾ cups button mushrooms, cleaned

1 tbsp chopped parsley

sea salt

freshly ground black pepper

Prep and cook time: 3 hour 30 minutes

Makes: 4 servings

1   Preheat the oven to 170°C (150° fan) | 325F | gas 3.

2   Heat 2 tbsp oil in a large pan and sear the meat in batches until browned all over. Set aside.

3   Add the rest of the oil to the pan and gently fry the shallots and bacon until lightly browned.

4   Add the garlic and return the meat to the pan. Stir in the flour and cook for 2 minutes.

5   Pour in the wine and stock and bring to a boil, stirring frequently. Add the carrots, thyme, and bay leaves, and season with salt and pepper.

6   Transfer to an ovenproof dish and bake in the oven for 2 ½ hours until the meat is very tender.

7   Melt the butter in a pan set over a medium heat and gently cook the mushrooms until browned. Add to the meat and cook in the oven for a further 30 minutes.

8   Remove from the oven and let stand briefly before serving with a sprinkle of chopped parsley.

Moroccan bean stew

Ingredients:
2 tbsp sunflower oil
1 large onion, finely chopped
2 cloves garlic, minced
2 tbsp fresh ginger, peeled and minced
1 tsp ground cinnamon
4 tsp ground cumin
1 tsp ground coriander
1 tsp smoked paprika
¼ tsp red chilli powder
3 cardamom pods, lightly crushed
2 tbsp harissa, North African spice paste
400 g | 14 oz | 1 ¾ cups tinned red kidney beans, drained and rinsed

400 g | 14 oz | 1 ¾ cups tinned chickpeas, drained and rinsed
400 g | 14 oz | 1 ¾ cups tinned butter beans, drained and rinsed
800 g | 28 oz | 4 cups tinned chopped tomatoes
2 tbsp lemon juice
2 tbsp pomegranate molasses
plain yoghurt, to serve
1 handful coriander, chopped
sea salt
freshly ground black pepper

Prep and cook time: 1 hour 20 minutes
Makes: 4 servings

1   Heat the oil in a casserole dish set over a medium heat. Add the onion, garlic, ginger and a pinch of salt, sweating until softened, 6–8 minutes.

2   Stir in the spices and harissa paste, cooking for 2 minutes until slightly darkened. Stir in the kidney beans, chickpeas, butter beans, chopped tomatoes and some salt and pepper to taste.

3   Bring to the boil and then reduce to a simmer until thickened, about 30–45 minutes; stir from time to time.

4   When ready, stir in the lemon juice, pomegranate molasses, and some more salt and pepper to taste.

5   Divide between bowls and top with yoghurt and coriander before serving.

'What to do with a difficult dining companion?'

We've known them for years; we're fond of them (we might even be related to them), but they have a tendency to get worked up about certain topics. They raise their voice; they speak too fast; they give the impression that they're taking on the whole world; they hardly seem to notice us anymore. The ranter can come across as sure of themselves: they know they're right and everyone on the other side is a fool or a fraud. It can be tedious.

In order to deal with the ranting person, it's crucial to analyse where their behaviour springs from. Often, it has little to do with the subject the ranter pursues with such vehemence: it isn't really about the crooked politicians, the injustice of the taxation system or the decline in manners among the young. In fact, a rant is an expression of desperation and a fiendishly disguised plea for love, tenderness and recognition.

What the ranting person needs above anything else is comfort and reassurance. They aren't mean so much as hurt and inwardly slighted. In terms of food, they benefit from dishes that evoke sweetness and generosity. This is akin to giving a friend a well-chosen present: the present can't ensure friendship on its own, but it exerts a limited yet genuine influence. With the right foods, expect the ranting to subside, one mouthful at a time.

Sweet potato and coconut curry

Ingredients:

2 tbsp sunflower oil
1 tsp mustard seeds
½ tsp cumin seeds
1 large onion, chopped
2 cloves garlic, minced
1 tbsp fresh ginger, minced
2 small red chillies, finely chopped
2 tsp mild curry powder
2 tsp ground coriander
1 tsp ground cumin
1 tsp ground turmeric
1 pinch sugar
3 large sweet potatoes, peeled
and diced

2 vine tomatoes, cored and puréed in
a food processor
300 ml | 11 fl oz | 1 ⅓ cups vegetable
stock
300 ml | 11 fl oz | 1 ⅓ cups coconut milk
½ lemon, juiced
coriander leaves, to garnish
sea salt
freshly ground black pepper

Prep and cook time: 50 minutes
Makes: 4 servings

1   Heat the oil in a large casserole dish set over a medium heat. Add the seeds, onion, garlic, ginger, chillies, and a pinch of salt, sweating for 8–10 minutes until softened and turning golden.

2   Stir in the spices and sugar, and cook for a further 2 minutes, stirring frequently, until the oil starts to bubble up from beneath the spices.

3   Stir in the sweet potatoes, puréed tomatoes, stock, and coconut milk. Bring to the boil and then reduce to a steady simmer.

4   Cook over a reduced until the sweet potatoes are tender to the tip of a knife, about 20–25 minutes; stir from time to time.

5   Adjust the seasoning to taste with lemon juice, salt, and pepper.

6   Ladle into bowls and serve with a garnish of coriander on top.

Orange and polenta cake

Ingredients:

For the cake:

3 free-range eggs

110 g | ½ cup caster sugar

110 g | ½ cup butter, melted and cooled

½ orange, juice and finely grated zest

225 g | 1 ½ cups polenta

½ tbsp baking powder

1 pinch salt

1 tsp vanilla extract

For the syrup:

3 oranges, juice

1 orange, coarsely grated zest

150 g | ⅔ cup caster sugar

Prep and cook time: 1 hour 25 minutes

Makes: 1 cake, approx. 12 servings

1   For the cake: heat the oven to 160°C (140° fan) | 325°F | gas 3. Grease a 20cm | 8" springform cake tin and line the base with non-stick baking paper.

2   Whisk the eggs and sugar with an electric whisk until thick and mousse like. Beat in the melted butter, orange juice and zest. Add the polenta and baking powder, salt and vanilla, beating well.

3   Pour into the tin and bake for 30–40 minutes until golden. Test by inserting a skewer or wooden cocktail stick, which should come out clean.

4   For the syrup: put all the ingredients into a pan and heat gently until the sugar has dissolved completely. Bring to a boil and simmer for 5 minutes. Make holes in the cake with a skewer. Pour over the hot syrup and zest and leave to cool completely until the syrup is absorbed, before removing from the tin.

Teasing done with affection and skill is a profound human accomplishment. There's nasty teasing, in which we pick away at a sore spot in someone's life. But there is a genuinely affectionate version, generous and loving, which feels good and instructive to be on the receiving end of.

All of us get a bit unbalanced in one way or another: too serious, too gloomy, too jokey. So we all benefit from being tugged back towards a healthier mean by a well-aimed, tenderly delivered tease. The good teaser latches onto and responds to our quirks and gets compassionately constructive about trying to reconnect us with our better selves – not by delivering a stern lesson, but by helping us to notice our excesses and laugh at them. We sense the teaser trying, with love, to give us a useful shove in a good (and secretly welcome) direction.

The best teasing remarks emerge from genuine insights into who we are. A person has studied us, put their finger on a struggle that's going on in us, and has taken the part of the highest, but currently under-supported, side of us.

It's especially charming to see someone who is in a position of power and authority being teased by their old friends. A stranger would probably be intimidated, but someone who knows them well might pretend there's a spider on their hair to puncture the grand exterior, because they know from experience that there's a childish, playful side to this individual, which needs encouragement. Teasing restores balance: it edges the intellectual to remember their taste for horseplay; the over-cautious to reconnect with their covert longings for adventure.

Teasing is a subtle, powerful mode of teaching. It builds on an important insight about human beings: criticism of any kind is hard to absorb; we are slow and reluctant learners with tendencies to ignore and turn against those who try to lecture us. By amusingly exaggerating our exaggerations, teasing combines criticism with charm. The negative point is real, but it is wrapped in kindness and disguised as entertainment, and is therefore much easier to take on board. It seduces us into virtue. ('If you want to tell people the truth, make them laugh, otherwise they'll kill you', advised George Bernard Shaw.)

Perhaps the most instructive question we can ask – the one that teaches us most about the value of affectionate teasing and of the path we still need to take towards emotional maturity – is simply: what do I need to be teased about?

Good teasing over a meal develops a feeling of equality. A big communal dish of seafood fritto misto, for instance, with shared dips (especially mayonnaise) can be an ideal accompaniment. If someone takes a piece you had your eye on, you might just lean over and grab it from their plate when they're not looking.

Seafood fritto misto

Ingredients:

1 ½ l | 53 fl oz | 6 cups vegetable oil
250 g | 9 oz | 2 cups plain flour
16 fresh sardines, cleaned, gutted,
and with heads removed
300 g | 11 oz | 2 cups fresh prawns,
peeled and deveined
300 g | 11 oz | 2 cups scallops, cleaned
with roe removed
300 g | 11 oz | 2 cups fresh squid tubes,
cleaned and cut into thin rings

1 handful flat-leaf parsley, chopped
tartar sauce, to serve
1 lemon, cut into wedges
sea salt
freshly ground black pepper

Prep and cook time: 20 minutes
Makes: 4 servings

1   Heat the oil in a large heavy-based saucepan to 180°C | 350F, using a thermometer to accurately gauge the temperature.

2   In the meantime, place the flour in a shallow dish and season with plenty of salt and pepper. Season the fish and seafood with plenty of salt and pepper as well.

3   When the oil is ready, add each individual seafood to the flour, in batches, tossing to coat. Deep-fry in batches until golden-brown and crisp, about 20–30 seconds per batch.

4   Using a slotted spoon, remove to a large tray lined with kitchen paper to drain, loosely covering with aluminium foil to keep warm. Repeat for the remaining batches.

5   When ready, serve with a garnish of parsley, some tartar sauce, and lemon wedges on the side for squeezing over.

'How lovely a bit of formality
can be …'

Sometimes, domestic life seems unfortunately squalid. Everyone has been shouting at everyone else. There's mess everywhere. No one is making any effort. People are sharing their most honest and ungenerous thoughts without making any attempt to censor themselves. There's too much swearing and quite a bit of slouching too.

It's time to use food to change the atmosphere; to introduce a note of formality that can jog us into remembering not to be fully 'ourselves'. Being formal can sound hypocritical, because it involves editing our thoughts and emotions before expressing them – but perhaps it is never very generous or kind to share the whole of our being with those around us.

We know all about the pleasures of informality, of letting ourselves laze around, of snacking on the sofa, of not worrying if we make a mess, munching on a toasted sandwich in our dressing gown or scooping ice cream straight from the tub. But there's another, contrastive, pleasure we may be neglecting: that of dressing up and attempting to be a bit elevated. We're no longer

being forced to do this by draconian social conventions. We're doing it because it's occasionally a relief to re-encounter our more civilised selves. We're tidying up, organising, making ourselves a bit smarter and crisper. We'll be polite; we'll ask proper questions; we won't chew and speak at the same time; we'll listen. We're telling ourselves something it's important to hear from time to time: we can master our impulses; we can control our actions; we can moderate our tone and select our words.

There are dishes, such as quail or oysters, that have a degree of dignity in their appearance, a certain delicacy of flavour, and whose consumption is a touch intricate. The cultural associations help as well: these foods are traditionally linked to solemn, ritualised occasions. Of course, the spread of casual dining has been of real benefit, and we should pride ourselves on having done away with the snobbery and pomposity of previous ages. It's an advance that we can admit how much we all enjoy a club sandwich. But there are moments when we remember why our forebears sometimes felt a craving for deliberately fancy, rule-bound

occasions. They wanted to create
a little distance between themselves
and the more savage sides of
existence.

Quails or oysters won't actually force
anyone not to say the first unpleasant
thing that flits through their head, but
they should hold them back a little,
especially if there are candles on the
table and we've brought out the fancy
linen napkins.

Roast quail

Ingredients:
2 cloves garlic, finely chopped
1 lemon, zest only, finely grated
1 small bunch flat-leaf parsley,
chopped
3 tbsp olive oil
4 quail, cleaned and trimmed
sea salt
freshly ground black pepper

Prep and cook time: 30 minutes
Makes: 4 servings

1   Preheat the oven to 200°C (180° fan) | 400F | gas 6.

2   Stir together the garlic, lemon zest, parsley and olive oil in a mixing bowl. Season the insides and outsides of the quail with salt and pepper.

3   Arrange the quail in a roasting dish before brushing the oil mixture onto their skins.

4   Roast until the thickest part of the thighs register at least 70°C | 160F on a meat thermometer, about 14–18 minutes usually.

5   Remove from the oven and let rest, loosely covered with aluminium foil, for at least 10 minutes before serving with roasted vegetables or with a little aioli (p. 105).

'If only we could all live
together ...'

Most of the eating that goes on happens alone in couples or in small groups. Recipes generally cater for four, or a maximum of eight. This reflects a general bias in modern society towards the atomised individual.

But there's a side of us that might imagine a more communal kind of life; one where we know all the neighbours on our street, where large cities are no longer so anonymous, where the emphasis is not invariably on couples and nuclear families (with all their tensions and squabbles) – and where we can regularly break bread at long tables of warm-hearted strangers.

In *The Republic*, the philosopher Plato (b. 429 BCE) imagined his ideal city anchored around a ritual of collective eating. Every evening, we'd sit at communal tables; rich and poor would share the same dishes; we'd get to know people very different from us; ideas would be passed from one generation to the next, and a sense of loyalty would gradually grow up where previously there had been only suspicion and fear.

Maybe we'd not really want this all the time, but such a vision speaks

to an often undernourished part of who we are: creatures who for millennia lived in large groups and benefited hugely from doing so. The life of couples and small family units is a recent phenomenon and a not untroubling one. It's only in the last few minutes, in historical terms, that we've taken our meals at little tables of two or four, shared news on our office lives, argued a bit, then quickly retired to our rooms to read a book or tap on our phones.

We've lost out: there's a liberating energy that arises from being a participant at a well-populated table. We can shed our anxieties and self-consciousness in the presence of a large number of kindly others who are ready to share with us some of their ideals and vulnerabilities. Perhaps many revolutions started because, at base, people were simply tired of eating every night with their spouse and craved to get out a bit and live on a more generous, communal footing.

But what would one eat in a utopian community setting? The ideal would be something simple, cheap and easy to make in large quantities. We'd dip into vast pots, pass around brimming jugs and laden dishes – and feel, at long last, the consoling pleasures of swapping the exhausting 'I' for the redemptive membership of a group.

Tarka dahl

Ingredients:

500 g | 1 lb | 2 ½ cups mung dahl
½ tsp turmeric
3 tbsp ghee
4 small onions finely sliced
1 tbsp cumin seeds
5 cloves of garlic minced
2 green chillis, slit lengthways
1 tsp mustard seeds
Handful chopped coriander

Prep and cook time: 1 hour 30 minutes
Makes: 10 servings

1   Rinse the dahl until the water runs clear.

2   Put the dahl and turmeric in the largest pan you have and cover with about 2–3 litres of water. If your pan isn't large enough, add the water in stages whilst cooking, making sure to check that the dahl is not drying out. Bring to the boil, skimming off any froth that forms of the surface. Turn down to a simmer.

3   While the dahl is cooking heat half the ghee in a frying pan over a medium high heat and add the onion and cumin seeds. Cook until lightly golden, then add half the minced garlic. Fry for another 1–2 minutes until the garlic is soft. Stir through the dahl.

4   Cook over a low heat for at least an hour until the dahl is soft and creamy. Add a little more water if the mix is too thick. Season with salt to taste. Remove from the heat.

5   Heat the remaining ghee in a pan and fry the mustard seeds until they start to pop, then add the green chillis and remaining garlic. Cook until lightly golden and then pour the hot ghee mixture over the cooked dahl. Garnish with chopped coriander.

Chapati

Ingredients:

140 g | 5 oz | 1 cup wholemeal flour

140 g | 5 oz | 1 cup plain flour, plus extra for dusting

1 tsp salt

3 tbsp sunflower oil, plus extra for greasing

180 ml | 6 fl oz | 1 cup warm water or as needed

Prep and cook time: 30 minutes

Makes: 10 servings

1   Stir together the flours and salt in a large bowl. Add 2 tablespoons of oil and water. Mix together to make a soft dough that isn't too sticky.

2   Tip the dough on to a lightly floured surface and kneed for 5–10 mins until smooth. Roll into a sausage shape and cut into 10 even pieces. Roll each piece into a ball and leave to rest for a few minutes.

3   Place a pan over medium heat and grease with a little of the remaining oil. Roll out the balls of dough into 20 cm | 8" rounds.

4   When the pan starts smoking, put a chapati on it. Cook on one side for about 30 seconds, then flip and cook on the other side. The chapati should have brown spots and be slightly puffed. Put on a plate and keep warm while you cook the rest of the chapatis.

Tomato chutney

Ingredients:
5–6 tomatoes
2 tbsp sunflower oil
½ tsp mustard seeds
2–3 dried red chillies
2 curry leaves
1 large onion, chopped fine
1 tsp salt
½ tsp brown sugar

Prep and cook time: 30 minutes
Makes: 4 servings

1   Score a cross into the bottom of each tomato. Bring a large pot of water to boil. Add the tomatoes to the water and boil for 30–60 seconds. Lift out and immediately plunge into ice cold water. Skin and leave until completely cool.

2   Put the cooled tomatoes in a food processor and puree, or grind to a smooth paste in a pestle and mortar.

3   Heat oil in a small pan over a high heat and add mustard seeds. A few seconds later add the chillies and curry leaves, once fragrant (10 seconds or so) add the onion. Fry until soft.

4   Add the pureed tomatoes, salt, sugar and about 100 ml | ½ cup of water.

5   Simmer for around 10–15 minutes, until the flavours have married.

4

Relationships

Relationships

Our intimate relationships are, theoretically, *the* source of comfort and connection. Our Romantic heritage suggests that if we can only find the right person, we will be guaranteed life-long satisfaction. It is a powerful fantasy.

But the reality is that almost all relationships are troubled and difficult; that probably no one will hurt us more than the person we dedicate our lives to, and vice versa. We may help each other in many ways, but even with the most delightful-seeming person, there will be areas of conflict and disappointment.

A more Classical view takes this for granted, so focuses on a range of skills and ideas that can help us to cope tolerably well with the unavoidable problems of love.

Food matters in relationships because it is a vehicle by which we can make psychological adjustments: we can foreground certain feelings; we can promote particular attitudes. Via a dish, we can launch an important conversation or recover our better selves after a setback; we can make a gesture of reconciliation or offer a sincere apology; we can invite a sensual mood or get to grips with an upsetting pattern of behaviour.

Food is crucial because so often words on their own are not enough. Food engages with the emotional part of our minds; it can bypass a rational disagreement or an entrenched logical argument. It doesn't directly say anything, but it warms, comforts, soothes, teases and charms. It is a critical ingredient that can help remind us to cherish one another as we should – and deep down perhaps always do.

'What could I prepare for a
dinner date?'

We've recently met someone and invited them around for dinner. There are many, varied bits of advice in circulation: don't do all the talking; be funny and light; avoid anything that might splash sauce on you or them; ask them about themselves; don't pry; be careful with garlic; wear nice shoes.

We're understandably nervous. We are trying to do something that is strange and tricky: to seduce another person. Not so much in the narrow and (potentially sinister) sense of trying to beguile them into bed, but in a larger, more fundamental way of getting them to like us.

A date is, in essence, an audition. Much more than we usually admit, we're trying to imagine each other as prospective long-term partners. Seduction, in its larger and more important sense, means gradually persuading someone that we're a plausible candidate with whom to be in a relationship.

The question then is: what are the things that might show us in this light? What do we need to do to get them on board?

There are two central priorities. The first is to show that we have a good relationship to ourselves. This doesn't involve saying how wonderful we are or what exciting lives we lead. We don't need to prepare anything obviously extraordinary. Our culture hints that it might be seductive to say things like 'I love Paris's museums' or 'I can rustle up an excellent bouillabaisse'. But such statements don't convey that we will be pleasant (or even bearable) to live with day to day.

On the contrary, what makes us attractive as a potential partner is the degree to which we can recognise our own failings. It's not that we should exhibit our flaws: getting furious when the pasta boils for too long, for example, or starting to weep about an old friend who let us down, or going on throughout the first course about an insult at work that happened years ago. This is weakness unbound and given total victory.

What is really sweet and charming – and powerfully reassuring – is weakness handled strongly. For instance, it might be seductive to drop in, with an air of confidence and wit: 'I didn't know whether I'd dare to introduce you to this pasta recipe; it's one my mum taught me when I was a kid, and I worried you might think it eerie or regressive to serve it tonight'. That's a sign both of insight and strength. We're not simply being nervous; we are vulnerable but have an overview on our anxieties and the capacity to handle them lightly.

The second seductive move is to signal that we view the other person with a mixture of tenderness and realism. It's often imagined that it will be seductive to convey an air of adoration, to hint that the other strikes us as exceptionally attractive or accomplished. But surprisingly, it is worrying to be obviously adored, because everyone, from the inside, knows that they don't deserve intense acclaim and are often broken or simply pitiful.

The seductive move is to suggest both that one likes the other person and yet can see their frailty; that one can cope with it and forgive it with gentle indulgence. One might, towards the end of the evening, drop in a small warm tease that alludes to our understanding of some less than perfect side of them: 'I suppose you stayed under the duvet feeling a bit sorry for yourself after that?' we might ask, with a benign smile.

Such a gesture implies that we genuinely like another person, not under a mistaken notion that they are flawless, but with a full and unfrightened appreciation of their frailties. That ends up being seductive because it is reassuring. It suggests the ideal way that we would like someone to view us within the testing conditions of a real relationship. We crave not admiration, but to be known and yet still liked and forgiven.

Many things are in the moment exciting, but self-knowledge and perceptive generosity are the most seductive things in the world; they are what makes life with another person bearable. They indicate that we have what it takes to embark on the long, exciting, beautiful and intermittently painful journey beyond the first date.

Prawn, garlic and lemon tagliatelle

Ingredients:
12 large shell-on king prawns
200 g dried tagliatelle
3 tbsp extra-virgin olive oil
2 garlic cloves, minced
1 fresh red chilli, deseeded and sliced
Finely grated zest 1 lemon plus the juice from one half
Large handful fresh parsley, roughly chopped

Prep time: 15 minutes
Cook time: 10 minutes
Makes: 2 servings

1   Prepare the prawns by removing the head and legs. Peel and discard the shell but keep the tails intact. Run a small sharp knife down the middle of the back to remove the dark vein. Rinse gently.

2   Cook the tagliatelle in a large saucepan of salted, boiling water until just tender to the bite (*al dente*), about 10 minutes.

3   While the pasta is cooking, heat 1 tablespoon of oil in a pan. When hot add the prawns, season well and cook for 2 minutes on one side. Flip over to cook on the other side, adding the rest of the oil, garlic, chilli, lemon zest and juice. Cook for another 2 minutes until the prawns are fully cooked through.

4   Drain the pasta and transfer into the prawn pan, coating everything in the flavoured oil. Divide between two plates and garnish with parsley.

What is really sweet
and charming – and
powerfully reassuring
– is weakness
handled strongly.

Chocolate mousse

Ingredients:
60 g | 2 oz dark chocolate, (min. 70% cocoa) roughly chopped
15 ml | 1 tbsp rum (optional)
2 eggs

Prep and cook time: 15 minutes
Chilling time: 2 hours
Makes: 2 servings

1   Melt the chocolate in a heatproof bowl over a pan of simmering (not boiling) water. Add the rum if using. Take off the heat and allow to cool slightly.

2   Separate the eggs. Beat the yolks and stir in the melted chocolate until smooth and glossy.

3   Whisk the egg whites into stiff peaks. Stir in a tablespoon of the whipped whites into the chocolate mixture and then carefully fold in the rest with a metal spoon until just combined.

4   Spoon the mousse into two pots and chill for at least 2 hours before serving.

'How can I soothe my unrequited passion?'

The pain of unrequited love is often accompanied by a certainty that if only the elusive target of our affection would return our smiles, come for dinner with us or marry us, we would know bliss. Total happiness seems tantalisingly close, wholly real and yet maddeningly out of reach.

At such moments, we are often counselled to go out, drink and try to forget the beloved. Given their lack of interest, we should try to think of something or someone else. Yet this kind counsel is misguided. The cure for love does not lie in ceasing to think of the fugitive lover, but in learning to think more intensely and constructively about who they might really be.

We should stay at home and prepare ourselves some fish – an ingredient perfectly suited to accompany salt tears. As we eat (perhaps black bream), we should remember that, close up, every human proves challenging. We are all trying propositions. We are short-tempered, vain, deceitful, crass, sentimental, woolly, cold, over-emotional and chaotic. What prevents us from holding this in mind in relation to the person we love from afar is simply a lack of knowledge.

We assume – on the basis of a few charming outside details – that the target of our passion may miraculously have escaped the fundamentals of the human condition. They haven't; we just haven't got to know them properly. This is what makes unrequited love so intense, so long-lasting and so vicious. By preventing us from growing close to them, the beloved also prevents us from tiring of them in the cathartic and liberating manner that is the gift of requited love.

It isn't their charms that keep us magnetised; it is our lack of knowledge of their flaws. The cure for unrequited love is therefore simple: we must get to know them better. The more we discover of them, the less they would look like the solution to all our problems. We would discover the endless small ways in which they are irksome; we'd get to know how stubborn, critical, cold and how hurt by things that strike us as meaningless they can be. If we got to know them better, we'd realise how much they had in common with everyone else.

Passion cannot withstand too much exposure to the full reality

of another person. The admiration
on which it is founded is destroyed
by the knowledge that a shared
life inevitably brings. The cruelty of
unrequited love isn't that we haven't
been loved back; it's that our hopes
have been aroused by someone who
can never disappoint us; someone
who we will have to keep believing in
because we lack the knowledge that
would set us free. In the absence of
a direct cure, we must undertake an
imaginative one. Without knowing
the details, we must accept that they
would eventually prove irritating:
everyone does. We have to believe
this not because we know it exactly of
them, but because they are human,
and we know this dark but cheering
fact about everyone who has ever
lived.

Black bream baked in a salt crust

Ingredients:

1 black bream, ready prepared
4 sprigs fresh parsley
1 tsp dried thyme
½ tsp dried rosemary
1 ½ kg coarse sea salt
4 egg whites
pepper
1 unwaxed lemon, in wedges

Prep and cook time: 1 hour
Makes: 2 servings

1 Rinse the fish and pat dry. Season the inside and outside of the fish with pepper. Wash the parsley, shake dry then place inside the belly cavity of the fish.

2 Heat the oven to 220°C (200° fan) | 425F | gas 7.

3 Place the thyme, rosemary and salt in a large bowl, whisk the egg white, then fold into the salt. Add a little water if necessary. Place half of the salt mixture on a baking tray lined with baking paper and put the fish on top. Now cover the fish with the remaining salt mixture. Press the mixture down firmly and smooth to seal any cracks.

4 Bake in the oven for 25–30 minutes. Crack the salt crust to reveal the tender steamed fish within. Serve with a green bean salad (see next page) and lemon wedges.

Green bean salad

Ingredients:
150 g | 5 oz green beans, trimmed
1 tbsp extra-virgin olive oil
juice of ½ lemon
1 tsp dijon mustard
6–8 cherry tomatoes, halved
½ small red onion, thinly sliced
sea salt
freshly ground black pepper
30 g | 1 oz feta (optional)

Prep and cook time: 30 minutes
Chill time: 1 hour
Makes: 2 servings

1   Bring a large pot of water to boil. Add the beans and cook for 4–5 minutes until tender.

2   Drain the beans and quickly refresh in some cool water. Drain again and set aside in a bowl with the sliced onion.

3   Whisk together the oil, lemon juice and mustard and pour over the beans and onion. Leave to marinate in the fridge for at least 1 hour. Add the tomatos and season just before serving. Scatter over some feta for an extra salty hit.

'What is true love?'

Curiously, we speak of love as one thing rather than discerning the two different varieties that lie beneath a single word: being loved and loving. It appears that we can only make a relationship work when we are ready to do the latter and are aware of our unnatural, immature fixation on the former. One of the greatest signs of the latter is knowing how to bring our partner something to eat in bed – on a tray, as a parent probably once did when we were little.

We start knowing only about being loved. It comes to seem wrongly like the norm. To the child, it feels as if the parent is simply spontaneously on hand to comfort, guide, entertain, feed and clear up while remaining almost always warm and cheerful. Parents generally don't reveal how often they've bitten their tongue, fought back tears, or been too tired to take off their clothes after a day of childcare. They simply bring us the tray of food and set it quietly on the bedside table next to us, and stroke our brow.

We learn of love in an entirely non-reciprocal context. The parent loves but they don't expect the favour to be returned in any significant way. The parent doesn't get upset when the child doesn't say an enormous thank you for the dinner or suggest that the parent now go upstairs and take a much-needed nap. Parent and child may both love, but each party is on a different end of the axis – unbeknown to the child.

This is why in adulthood, when we first say we long for love, what we predominantly mean is that we want to be loved as we were once loved by a parent. We want a recreation in adulthood of what it felt like to be administered to and indulged. In a secret part of our minds, we picture someone who will understand our needs, bring us whatever we want, be immensely sympathetic and patient towards us, act selflessly and make many things better.

This is a disaster for our unions. For any relationship to work, we need to move firmly out of the position of the child and into that of the parent. We need to become someone who can sometimes subordinate their own demands to the needs of another.

To be adults in love, we have to learn to do something remarkable: to put someone else ahead of us,

probably by bringing them something
succulent to eat on a tray.

Baked eggs with buttered soldiers

Ingredients:

2 tbsp butter + extra for toast
2 eggs
2 tbsp cream
2 handfuls of grated hard cheese
such as Parmesan
salt
freshly ground black pepper
Optional extras such as cooked ham,
cooked mushrooms, chives

To serve:

Wholemeal bread, toasted and sliced
into soliders

Prep and cook time: 10 minutes
Makes: 2 servings

1   Heat oven to the highest setting.

2   Butter two ramekins generously; if you're using any extra ingredients place
into the bottom of the dish.

3   Crack an egg in each ramekin, top generously with cheese and cream.

4   Cook for approx. 8–10 minutes until white is set and yolks are runny.
Serve with buttered soliders.

Blueberry pancakes

Ingredients:
175 ml | 6 fl oz | ¾ cup milk
2 tbsp white vinegar
100 g | 4 oz | ¼ cup self raising flour
2 tbsp caster sugar
1 tsp baking powder
1 egg
25 g | 2 tbsp melted butter, plus a little
extra for the pan
2 handfuls fresh blueberries

Prep and cook time: 15 minutes
Makes: 2 servings

1   Mix the milk and vinegar and set aside for a minute.

2   Sift the dry ingredients together into a bowl. Make a well and then whisk in the egg, milk and melted butter until combined into a smooth batter.

3   Melt a little butter in a pan over a medium heat.

4   Pour batter into the pan to form a thick pancake approximately 8 cm | 3" in diameter.

5   Dot blueberries on top. Cook until small bubbles start to appear on top of the pancake (about 2–3 minutes). Flip and cook for another 1–2 minutes until the pancakes are fluffy and golden.

6   Serve with butter and maple syrup.

It's a sign of being a grown-up that we can admit that we are difficult to live with.

'How can I reintroduce good will
into my relationship?'

None of us need partners who are perfect. What we need above all is a sense that others understand their imperfections, that they are ready to explain them calmly, and that they can do so outside of the moments when they have behaved badly.

It's a sign of being a grown-up that we can admit that we are difficult to live with. Everyone is. It's just a question of how we, in particular, are tricky.

We should regularly prepare something soothing – and, as we eat together, go over some of the things we most regret doing in our relationship.

We might, for instance, admit that we do have slightly mad views about interior design and find any opposition to our taste distressing in ways that must be annoying. Or we can confess that we are fanatically devoted to our work. We can apologise that we have such strong views on how long it is OK to keep a taxi waiting, whether bedroom windows should be kept open at night, or what time a child needs to go to bed (to start sketching a potentially endless list).

Recognising where we are inflexible and where we are demanding won't solve all the points of contention, but it can change the atmosphere. We should never be done with the business of apologising for how challenging we are to be around.

Dorset pork and cider casserole
with mustard and sage

Ingredients:
2 tbsp sunflower oil, divided
150 g | 5 oz | 1 cup pancetta, or bacon
lardons, cubed
1.2 kg | 42 oz pork shoulder, trimmed
and cut into 5 cm | 2" pieces
4 tbsp butter
2 large onions, roughly chopped
2 tbsp plain flour
400 ml | 14 fl oz | 1 ⅔ cups cider,
preferably dry
400 ml | 14 fl oz | 1 ⅔ cups chicken
stock
2 tbsp sage, chopped; plus extra
to garnish
2 large celery stalks, roughly sliced
1 large carrot, roughly sliced
1 large apple, cored and diced
2 tbsp wholegrain mustard
3 tbsp double cream
salt
freshly ground black pepper

Prep and cook time: 2 hour 50 minutes
Makes: 4 servings

1   Preheat the oven to 170°C (150° fan) | 325F | gas 3.

2   Heat 1 tablespoon oil in a large casserole dish set over a medium heat until hot. Add the pancetta and fry until golden-brown, about 6–8 minutes. Using a slotted spoon, remove to a plate lined with kitchen paper to drain.

3   Add the remaining oil to the dish and increase the heat to moderate. Season the pork with salt and pepper and, working in batches, brown in the hot oil. Remove to the same plate as the pancetta.

4   Add 2 tablespoon butter to the dish followed by the onions, sautéing until golden, about 8–10 minutes. Sprinkle over the flour and cook for 2 minutes, stirring from time to time.

5   Return the pancetta and pork to the dish, and stir in the cider, stock and sage.

6   Bring to the boil, cover with a tight-fitting lid, and transfer to the oven, cooking for 1 ½ hours.

7   Remove from the oven and stir in the celery, carrot and apple. Cover and return to the oven for a further 30 minutes until the pork and vegetables are tender.

8   Remove from the oven and place over a medium-low heat. Whisk in the remaining butter, mustard and cream, returning to a simmer.

9   Season to taste with salt and pepper before serving with a garnish of sage.

Roasted aubergine curry with cooling coconut cream

Ingredients:
250 g | 1 ½ cups basmati rice
2 tbsp coriander seeds
1 tbsp cumin seeds
2 large banana shallots, finely chopped
3 garlic cloves, minced
2 green finger chillies, deseeded and finely chopped
1 thumb fresh ginger, ~ 5 cm | 2" in diameter, peeled and finely chopped
4 tbsp sunflower oil
1 tsp mild curry powder
2 tbsp red curry paste
400 ml | 14 fl oz coconut milk
1 large aubergine
1 lime
1 bunch Thai basil
flaked sea salt
freshly ground black pepper

Prep and cook time: 1 hour 5 minutes
Makes: 4 servings

1   Rinse and soak the rice in a bowl of lukewarm water.

2   Place the coriander and cumin seeds in a dry frying pan. Toast over a medium heat until fragrant.

3   Tip into a mortar and grind finely with a pestle.

4   Heat 2 tablespoons sunflower oil in a wok or high-sided sauté pan set over a moderate heat. Add the shallot, garlic and a pinch of salt, sautéing until softened. Stir in the chilli and ginger, and continue to sauté.

5   Stir in the ground spices, curry powder and curry paste. Cook for 2 minutes, stirring frequently, before stirring in the coconut milk. Bring to a simmer and cook steadily until slightly thickened, about 5 minutes. Season to taste with salt and pepper before setting aside.

6   Drain the rice. Bring 750 ml | 3 cups water to the boil in a heavy-based saucepan. Stir in 1 tsp salt and then the drained rice. Bring to the boil, cover with a lid, and cook over a low heat until the rice has absorbed the water and is tender to the bite, about 20–25 minutes. Remove from the heat and set aside to cool, still covered; fluff with a fork just before serving.

7   Cut the aubergine into long, thin slices approximately ½ cm | ¼" thick.

8   Brush a griddle pan with some of the remaining oil. Brush the aubergine slices with some oil and season with salt and pepper. Griddle in the pan until soft and lightly coloured on both sides, about 5–6 minutes in total.

9   Arrange the griddled aubergine in a serving dish. Reheat the sauce before ladling over the aubergine.

10   Pick the leaves from the basil sprigs. Halve and juice the lime, stirring some into the sauce to taste. Garnish the curry with the picked basil leaves and serve with a dish of the rice on the side.

'How can I graciously withdraw
from a sulk?'

We sulk out of a misplaced sense of hope. We go silent and refuse to say what is wrong because we expect that the other person should understand us *without us needing to spell things out.*

We remain silent and furiously gnomic because having to articulate the offence another has caused us feels contrary to the spirit of love, interpreted in a Romantic sense: if the other requires an explanation, it is proof that they are not worthy of being granted one. True love should, after all, be about mutual and speedy intuition, not laborious articulation.

This sounds logical, except for one thing: we're forgetting that the other person cannot magically know what's going on in our heads. Our feelings and thoughts are evident to us, but not to anyone standing outside of our minds.

Even though we feel justified in our fury, a small part of our mind knows that we are being childish. What we would most like is for this to end, but climbing down feels humiliating. We're not ready to resolve the issue in detail. We just want to get past it.

Food can offer a helpful manoeuvre. By offering our partner something to eat, we're breaking our hard silence. We're not directly admitting our madness or denying that we were offended, but we're acting in a warmer way. The ideal sulk-ending dish is one marked by a softness and ungrudging generosity that we're currently struggling to find in ourselves. It's our edible ambassador: something that can whisper about a reconciliation that we can't bring ourselves to mention directly.

It might be especially constructive to share the dish on the sofa while watching a favourite episode from a TV drama. We don't have to say much, but via what is on our plates, we're quietly re-establishing an underlying connection – and signalling that we will get through this.

Polenta with poached eggs

Ingredients:

300 ml | 10 fl oz | 1 ¼ cups whole milk
300 ml | 10 fl oz | 1 ¼ cups water
70 g | 2 ½ oz | ½ cup fine polenta, cornmeal
1 tbsp butter, cubed
1 tbsp Parmesan, grated
1 tbsp white wine vinegar
2 large eggs
extra-virgin olive oil, to serve

salt
freshly ground black pepper

Prep and cook time: 1 hour 20 minutes
Makes: 2 servings

1   Bring the milk and water to a rapid simmer in a large saucepan. Gradually whisk in the polenta to prevent the mixture from clumping. Once incorporated, bring the polenta to the boil until it starts to spit.

2   Once spitting, immediately reduce the heat to low and simmer very gently until thickened, about 40–50 minutes; stir with a spatula from time to time to prevent sticking.

3   When ready, whisk in the butter by the cube followed by the Parmesan and some salt and pepper to taste. Cover and keep warm off the heat.

4   Bring a large saucepan of water to a steady simmer over a medium heat. Stir in the vinegar and crack the eggs into small cups. Working quickly, slide the eggs into the simmering water, poaching for 3 minutes. Using a slotted spoon, remove the eggs to a plate lined with kitchen paper.

5   If needed, gently reheat the polenta. Divide between small bowls and top with poached eggs, seasoning them with salt and pepper. Drizzle with a little extra-virgin olive oil, salsa verde (p. 57) or pesto (p. 90) before serving.

It won't change everything, but the right dish can coax a more playful spirit closer to the front of our minds.

'We don't have fun any more …'

Ages ago, it feels, we used to have fun. We'd do some idiotic things together – irresponsible, childish or worse. We felt safe enough together to let the more playful, silly parts of who we are be evident. We could trust that our partner wouldn't hold it against us.

But being together over the long term transmutes into increased responsibility. An enduring relationship has certain important elements in common with setting up a small business together. Our lives become financially and practically intertwined. There are many serious decisions to be made. Even teasing gets harder, because there's a growing background of real criticism: what was once a throwaway remark now has an edge of accusation and bitterness to it.

Food has the power to trigger dormant emotions. Our brains wire emotional memories to sensations so we can use food to connect us back to states of mind we value from the past. It won't change everything, but the right dish can coax a more playful spirit closer to the front of our minds.

It's usefully entertaining to eat a fondue together. Using your skewers like miniature swords you both dunk cubes of bread into the molten mixture and see how long you can stretch the cheese before it snaps. You are being an idiot, of course. But you are – at last and again – being idiots together.

Fondue

Ingredients:

1 small clove garlic finely chopped
150 ml | 5 fl oz | ½ cup dry white wine
1 tsp lemon juice
125 g | 5 oz Emmental cheese grated
125 g | 5 oz Gruyère cheese grated
1 tsp cornflour
1 tbsp kirsch (optional)
Nutmeg, grated

To serve:

Cubed sourdough, for dipping

Prep and cook time: 30 minutes
Makes: 2 servings

1 Put the garlic, wine and lemon juice into a fondue pot and bring to a boil on the hob.

2 Turn down the heat and add the cheeses a little at the time. Whisk continually to avoid lumps.

3 Add the cornflour to the kirsch if using, otherwise just blend with cold water. Pour into the pot and cook gently for a few minutes until the mixture has thickened.

4 Season with a little nutmeg, and place the fondue pot over a flame at the table. Serve immediately.

'How can I remain patient
around my partner?'

Small children can behave in stunningly unfair ways: they scream at the person who is looking after them, angrily push away a bowl of pasta or throw away something you have just fetched for them. But we rarely feel agitated or wounded by their behaviour, because we don't assign a negative motive to a small person. We reach around for benevolent interpretations; they are probably tired, or their gums are sore, or they are upset by the arrival of a younger sibling. We've got a repertoire of alternative explanations ready, none of which lead us to panic or get agitated.

This is the reverse of what tends to happen around adults in general, and our lovers in particular. Here we imagine that others deliberately have us in their sights. If the partner is late for our mother's birthday because of 'work', we assume it's an excuse. If they promised to pick up some toothpaste but then 'forgot', we'll imagine a deliberate slight. But if we employed the infant model of interpretation, our first assumption would be different: maybe they didn't sleep well last night and are too exhausted to think straight; maybe they've got a sore knee; maybe they

are doing the equivalent of testing the boundaries of parental tolerance. Seen from this angle, adult behaviour doesn't magically become nice or acceptable, but the level of agitation is kept safely low. It's touching that we live in a world where we have learnt to be so kind to children: it would be even nicer if we learnt to be a more generous towards the childlike parts of one another.

We do our fellow adults the greatest possible favour when we are able to regard at least some of their bad behaviour as we would those of an infant. To help us do this, we should ask those we love to explain to us what food they liked when they were small, and then prepare these dishes when we risk seeing them only through intemperate adult lenses. We are so alive to the idea that it's patronising to be thought of as younger than we are, we forget that it is also, at times, the greatest privilege for someone to look beyond our adult self in order to engage with, forgive and sometimes cook for the testing but ultimately worthy child within.

Bread and butter pudding

Ingredients:
8 slices bread
55 g | ¼ cup butter
150 g | 1 cup raisins
1 tsp ground cinnamon
400 ml | 1 ⅔ cup milk
2 eggs
55 g | ¼ cup icing sugar

Prep and cook time: 1 hour 20 minutes
Makes: 4 servings

1   Lightly butter a 1 litre | 2 pint pie or baking dish.

2   Spread the butter on 1 side of each slice of bread and slice diagonally in half. Place a layer of bread, buttered-side up, in the base of the dish, then add a layer of raisins. Sprinkle with a little cinnamon, then repeat the layers of bread, raisins and a sprinkling of cinnamon, until all the bread is used. Finish with a layer of bread and set aside.

3   Gently warm the milk in a pan over a low heat to scalding point. Do not boil.

4   Beat the eggs with ¾ of the sugar and whisk until pale and frothy.

5   Add the warm milk and stir well, then pour the mixture over the bread layers and sprinkle with the remaining sugar. Leave to stand for 30 minutes.

6   Heat the oven to 180°C (160° fan) | 350°F | gas 4.

7   Cook for 30–40 minutes, until the custard has set and the top is golden brown. Sift a little icing sugar over the top.

'How can I remain grateful to
my partner?'

It's hard to keep it in mind, given
the pressures of most days and
the endless stream of small troubles,
but our partner really has helped
us in some major ways. Maybe it's
not anything they've done in the
last twenty-four hours, but across
the years, there are ways in which
they have made a huge contribution.
Perhaps they helped us get on top
of our finances; possibly they saved
us from the potential danger of
some unfortunate sides of our own
character; it could be that they were
gentle and kindly when we went
through a difficult period; maybe
they've been quietly encouraging
when we've been lacking confidence.
These are crucial elements in the
history of why we are together that
we often overlook.

We can deploy a special dish to make
a vital point: we're going out of our
way to remember what we're grateful
to the other for and why. We're
doing something unusual: putting a
spotlight on our debt to them. The
ideal dish would be something that's
delicious and evidently for a special
occasion.

As we buy the truffle and slowly
prepare the pasta, we're jogging our
own memories. When we present
them (perhaps as an unannounced
surprise) with a splendid offering,
we're making apparent to them that,
even though we often forget this, we
couldn't quite live without them.

Fresh egg pasta with shaved truffle

Ingredients:

For the pasta:

2 large free-range eggs

200 g | 1 ½ cups '00' flour

To serve:

75 g | ¾ cup Parmesan cheese, grated

100 g | ½ cup salted butter

25 g | 1 oz fresh black truffle

fresh parsley

salt

freshly ground black pepper

Prep and cook time: 15–20 minutes

Makes: 2 servings

1   To make the pasta place flour on a clean work surface, make a well and crack the eggs into it. Beat the eggs with a fork, incorporating the flour gradually until everything is bound together. Knead until smooth. Cover in clingfilm and rest for at least ½ hour in the fridge.

2   Dust the work surface with more flour and roll out the dough as thin as possible using a rolling pin. Alternatively, use a pasta machine. Working quickly, cut into wide flat strips and cover with a damp tea towel while you continue with the next steps.

3   Add the butter to a heavy based pan and let it melt over a low heat. Once melted grate in about ¾ of the black truffle. Stir well and then remove from the heat.

4   Drop pasta into boiling water and cook for around 3–4 minutes until just cooked. Reserve 120ml | ½ cup of the cooking water and then drain.

5   Stir the pasta into the butter, along with a little of the reserved water. Stir gently over a low heat until everything is combined. Add more water if it starts to feel sticky. Add the Parmesan and serve immediately. Garnish with fresh parsley and more shavings of black truffle.

Without being morbid or brutal, suppose that you never saw your partner again, and you were able to look back from a distance and think about your relationship. What would you miss?

Imagine that any hurt or shame has faded sufficiently and you can afford to admit there are things you would miss enormously about them. What would they be? We don't tend to carry such a list around with us at the front of our minds. It takes time to identify the things we would ache for and be sorry we had lost.

We don't need to wait for the passage of time. Instead we can, in our imaginations, propel ourselves into a possible future and from there try to imagine what we'd feel. The point is not so much to predict what we might miss as to get us to realise that those things are in our grasp right now.

Collect some of the dishes that mean the most to your partner: the one their mother used to make for them; the one they picked up living in Greece after university; the one they resort to when they are feeling sad and put upon … These dishes are emblems of a crucial idea: the good in your partner is always there, waiting for the right prompts to be noticed and savoured.

Make a note of your partner's
most meaningful dishes

The idea of starting afresh is often tempting: if only we could put aside the past hurts and frustrations and begin again with the wisdom we now have. We know so much more about ourselves and about being in a relationship than we did when the two of us had our first date. How would we now behave if we were to rerun the meal?

To lend the thought experiment more weight, we should every now and then go on a 'first date' with our partner. Even after years together, we should dress up and prepare a meal for them as if it were the first one.

How might we behave differently? We might feel that it would be important to explain certain aspects of ourselves with greater candour and emphasis. We might want to be more upfront and admit that we are difficult in certain ways, so that there wouldn't be a gradual unfolding of frustration and disappointment. Perhaps in this fantasised new first date, we'd be interested in getting to know quite different things about our partner. We'd maybe want to learn more about their childhood (especially its difficult parts, not just the happy memories).

Perhaps we might also want to be nicer and sweeter than we normally are. We might want to charm our partner, listen carefully to their ideas and opinions; we might be intrigued afresh by the way they fold their hands under their chin or by the ironic way they shrug their shoulders when telling a funny story. We'd be re-sensitised to a range of endearing qualities that have been neglected in the course of daily life.

The first date experiment gets us to see our partner afresh. What we see is part of who they really have been all the while. We're using a mealtime artifice to correct the fateful blindness and ingratitude of time.

Griddled asparagus

Ingredients:
230g | ½ lb asparagus, woody ends removed
1 tsp olive oil
1 lemon, halved
2 tbsp Parmesan, shaved
2 tbsp flaked almonds, toasted
sea salt
freshly ground black pepper

Prep and cook time: 15 minutes
Makes: 2 servings

1   Preheat a griddle pan over a medium heat and brush over a little olive oil.

2   Toss the asparagus in the remaining oil and place in the hot pan. cook for 5-7 minutes, shaking the pan every now and then.

3   Squeeze over the lemon juice and then transfer the asparagus to a serving platter.

4   Scatter over the Parmesan shavings and toasted almonds. Season to taste.

Grilled lobster

Ingredients:
150 g | ½ cup softened butter
2 tbsp finely chopped parsley
1 ½ tsp crushed red chilli flakes
4 cloves garlic, finely chopped
Zest of 1 lemon
Sea salt and freshly ground black
pepper, to taste
1 cooked lobster (about 600–900g |
1 ½–2 lb)
60 ml | ¼ cup olive oil

Prep time: 20 minutes
Cook time: 10 minutes
Makes: 2 servings (½ a lobster each)

1   Combine butter, parsley, chilli flakes, garlic, lemon zest, salt and pepper in a bowl; set aside.

2   Twist the claws off from the lobster. Crack the claws and remove the meat inside. Set to one side.

3   Cut the lobster in half. Rinse and dry the head cavity then fill with the claw meat. Lay the lobster halves, cut side up, in a shallow baking tray.

4   Heat grill to high. Baste the lobster meat generously with the flavoured butter. Grill for 5 minutes until the butter is bubbling and starting to brown. Plate the lobsters and serve with fries.

Tiramisu

Ingredients:

2 eggs, separated
2 tbsp caster sugar
100 g | 4 oz mascarpone
1 tbsp sweet marsala
1 tbsp dark rum
75 ml | 2 ½ fl oz | ⅓ cup espresso
6 ladies finger biscuits, each one
sliced into three equal sized pieces
Cocoa powder, to dust

Prep time: 15 minutes
Cool time: 3 hours
Makes: 2 servings

1   Whisk the egg whites until stiff, then set aside.

2   In a separate bowl whisk the egg yolks with the sugar until pale, then add the mascarpone a little at a time. Gently fold the egg whites into mixture with a large metal spoon until there is no visible white.

3   Put the marsala, rum and espresso in a shallow dish. Dip each sliced lady finger into the liquid then arrange to cover the bases of two individual trifle dishes. Spoon ⅓ of the mascarpone mixture on top of each of the dishes, followed by a little cocoa, then repeat the layers, finishing with a layer of the mascarpone and cocoa.

4   Cover and refrigerate for at least 3 hours before serving.

We're using a mealtime artifice to correct the fateful blindness and ingratitude of time.

5
Good
enough

Good Enough

In many areas of life, it's easy for us to feel that we have failed to live up to our own expectations. We are evidently not beautiful, rich, intelligent, kind or clever enough. In this context, nor are we anything like the sort of cooks we should be. We've seen the lovely illustrations in the glossy books; we may have equipped our kitchens with the right implements and crockery sets; we know a lot of people with impressive culinary skills; we know how it all ought to be. Yet our own efforts fail to rise up to the requisite standards. We feel ashamed and sorrowful about how bad we are at cooking.

This agonising gap between how we want to be and how we actually are was of great interest to Donald Winnicott (see p. 200). He was struck by the way that many well-intentioned, sincere and decent parents would come to his consulting room in distress. They were paralysed by the fear that they were doing so many things wrong in bringing up their children. They felt disgusted with themselves and, as a result, were unable to enjoy their roles or make even modest improvements to their techniques. To help these parents, Winnicott developed a concept of what he called the 'good enough' parent.

Of course, parents would make mistakes, he reassured them, but these were almost always far from serious. A child, he argued, doesn't need a perfect parent anyway. They can cope with an often kind, sometimes muddled, generally well-meaning and real human being: in other words, a 'good enough' parent.

A similar attack on vicious perfectionism needs to happen around food. We have been tortured for too long by images of flawless meals. We have come to hate our efforts, despise ourselves and refuse to let other people taste what we make, because we are haunted by glossy ideals. The desire to cook well has fatefully undermined our capacity to take pride in the decent, sometimes charming and at other points quite wonky results we are capable of.

Despite our insecurities and occasional kitchen fiascos, as Winnicott would surely have told us, we are 'good enough' cooks already. In the greater scheme, it doesn't matter that our meat is often over-cooked, our pasta is seldom *al dente* and our cakes look nothing like they should.

This section is a guide to, and celebration of, something that almost never makes it into cookbooks but is infinitely more important than the visions of manicured perfection they tease us with: flawed but good enough cooking and eating.

'I just can't cook!'

It can't be true.

A self-described inability to cook is always relative to some overly punishing internal vision of what 'cooking' means. A real cook, we tell ourselves, makes their own mayonnaise; they have a special way of washing and drying lettuce; they are obsessive about the quality of the knives they use; they always follow recipes precisely or they have invented their own wonderful variations drawn from trips abroad; they have a store cupboard full of things they prepared; they know how to bake bread; they can make a soufflé rise; they know about the quality of ingredients, and go to special shops to find exactly the right spices and vegetables; they don't get stressed at the stove; when they cook a chicken, the breast meat never goes dry.

By this standard, of course, we truly can't cook.

And yet we can. We can cook all sorts of things perfectly well, even if we don't get them exactly right. A fried egg is still delicious even if it goes a little crisp around the edges or if the yolk is over-cooked. We can still enjoy our pasta even if we did forget to salt the boiling water before putting in the spaghetti and some of it stuck to the bottom of the pan when we drained it. These dishes, and thousands more like them, tolerate a bit of erroneous handling. Like a good friend, they won't hold our slight mistakes against us. The ultimate goal is simply that we enjoy our meal.

What we're discussing here isn't just about cooking; we're telling ourselves a more universal truth via our modest adventures in the kitchen. The idea of being good enough is one that can be helpfully invoked in many areas. There's the good enough marriage, the good enough job, or the good enough holiday. A demanding vision of perfection isn't an avenue to great results or a better life: it is, on the contrary, pretty much a guarantee that we'll be and feel like failures. Our imperfectly arranged, slightly unevenly cooked and in places plain charred meals are a grand symbol of a big idea: a wise accommodation with the imperfect nature of reality.

Fried egg on toast

Ingredients:
1 free range egg, room temperature
1 tbsp olive oil
sea salt
black pepper

Prep and cook time: 5 minutes
Makes: 1 serving

To serve:
Bread of your choosing
A little butter

1   Place a small non-stick frying pan over a medium to low heat. Pour in a little oil and wait until it is hot enough to lightly coat the entire surface of the pan.

2   Crack the egg into the pan. Resist the urge to move the egg and instead wait until the white has set, about 3 minutes. If you prefer your eggs over-easy, flip towards the end of the cooking time.

3   While the egg is cooking, toast a slice of bread and generously butter.

4   Slide the cooked egg from the frying pan on to the toast. Serve with ketchup or top with salsa verde (p. 57) for an extra kick.

Cacio e Pepe

Ingredients:
450 g | 16 oz spaghetti
4 tbsp butter, divided
2 tbsp extra-virgin olive oil
2 tsp freshly ground black pepper, divided
200 g | 7 oz | 2 cups Parmesan, freshly grated

Prep and cook time: 20 minutes
Makes: 4 servings

1   Cook the spaghetti in a large saucepan of salted, boiling water until just tender to the bite (*al dente*), about 10–12 minutes.

2   Drain well, reserving about one small cup of the starchy cooking water.

3   Melt 2 tablespoons butter with the olive oil in a large sauté pan set over a medium heat until hot. Stir in 1 tsp black pepper and cook until fragrant, about 30 seconds.

4   Add about half the starchy cooking water, bringing to a simmer. Whisk in the remaining butter and then add the cooked spaghetti, tossing with tongs.

5   Gradually sprinkle in the Parmesan, tossing and stirring the spaghetti with the tongs to coat in the Parmesan and sauce.

6   Once a glossy, cheesy sauce forms, remove the pan from the heat and loosen the spaghetti with more cooking water, if needed.

7   Divide between plates or bowls and top with the remaining black pepper before serving.

'Am I allowed to order in?'

To go by most cookbooks, the idea of ordering in simply doesn't exist, not even as a concept. This is what barbarians and infidels might do after sacking a city.

However, ordering in has a legitimate and noble place within the repertoire of the ordinary, good enough, home cook. Knowing when not to cook is a skill requiring as much self-belief and emotional maturity as cooking itself.

For a start, to order in, we need to learn to like ourselves and accept that sometimes we deserve to let others help us. We have to come to terms with the concept of dependence, and the legitimacy of our own feelings of exhaustion. Perhaps we've simply done enough for now and need to let the Star of India or the Jade Garden do the work for a while. Asking for help, realising that one can't cope alone, is at times a genuinely wise piece of self-knowledge. We're admitting to ourselves (and a lot in our past might have made this hard) that we are allowed to be tired, fed up or depleted, and that these needn't be signs that we're shirking or lazy.

Perhaps we've had a reversal in our love life; perhaps work has been taxing; perhaps we couldn't sleep last night.... When we go to the door and take a bag from a helmeted bike delivery person, we're inducted to a general idea: we're entitled to be looked after sometimes. We can from time to time skip on certain duties and still be acceptable, honourable human beings.

We should feel no less ashamed to admit our weaknesses to others. Imagine that some old friends are coming round. Theoretically, we'd love to prepare something wonderful to charm and impress them. But we are exhausted and weepy. We want nothing more than to curl up in bed and be held. What should we do? We're operating under the punishing idea that our friends will like us only if we perform at our best, which here might mean unveiling a home-cooked pie or roast lemon and thyme chicken on a bed of rosemary potatoes. However, we're forgetting something crucial to friendship. Our friends like us despite, and in fact almost because of, our failings, weaknesses, incapacities and imperfections.

Being flawless would only serve to threaten and intimidate them. They would far rather connect with our vulnerability than be awed by our superiority.

Being impressive can win one admiration; however, it is by revealing our ordinary, broken selves that we create proper friendships. We should dare to take our friends into our darkened kitchen, while dressed in an old T-shirt and jeans, with tear stains around our eyes (we'll be ready to explain them soon), and declare without embarrassment that a large bag is currently on its way from Memories of Bengal. That is, in the deep sense, the beginning of true hospitality.

To go by most cookbooks, the idea of ordering in simply doesn't exist, not even as a concept. This is what barbarians and infidels might do after sacking a city.

'What can we do with leftovers?'

The standard answer is to tip them into the bin, like much that is flawed, imperfect and less-than-acceptable about human existence. However, the good enough cook knows that leftovers are a fundamental part of the weekly diet.

Viewed with sufficient creativity and free-spiritedness, there is something beguiling about stale bread, congealed steak, gelatinous beans and last night's half-eaten roast tomatoes.

The pleasure isn't just that they taste nice (often nicer than the first time around); such dishes hint at a bigger theme: the way that something that has been rejected can, in the right circumstances, become central and impressive. In religion, this idea crops up in the Gospel of St Matthew. In one of the parables, Jesus declares that 'the stone that the builders have rejected will become the cornerstone.' What he means is that 'leftover' people who are so often regarded as unworthy – the meek, the poor, the untalented – will one day have a completely different place in the Kingdom of God, where the secret merits of their souls will be recognised.

This idea stretches way beyond religion. In our own lives too, we can sometimes see that low-prestige things (the 'leftovers' of the predominant culture) can turn out to be lovely if we give them a chance. It might, for instance, seem that no one could ever want to go on holiday with their elderly aunt in a caravan. But it can be enormously pleasurable to spend time in an ingenious compact mobile home touring unexplored bits of the landscape with an aunt who, even though she dyes her hair badly and wears unflattering clothes, turns out to have an interesting past and intriguing views on literature and politics. Generosity of imagination is what we will all need someone to apply to us one day.

We too will, at some point, be a 'left over', a slightly dispiriting item in the back of the fridge of life – and we too will need others to come along and know how to perceive our potential beneath an unprepossessing exterior. When we make a pleasing meal the next day out of the things that were unwanted late last night, we're enacting one of the profoundest themes of existence: redemption.

Arancini

Ingredients:

Left over risotto – approx. 4 servings worth (see p. 129)

2 tbsp olive oil

1 large shallot, finely chopped

1 clove garlic, minced

400 g | 2 ½ cups beef mince

2 tbsp tomato puree

250 ml | 1 cup beef stock

150 g | 1 cup frozen peas, thawed

1 litre vegetable oil, for deep-frying

1 small bunch basil, leaves only, chopped

165 g | 1 ½ cups breadcrumbs

Prep and cook time: 30 minutes

Makes: 4 servings

1   Heat the olive oil in a large saucepan set over a medium heat. Add the shallot, garlic and a pinch of salt, sweating for 4–5 minutes until softened. Increase the heat a little and add the beef mince, browning well all over. Stir in the tomato puree, cook for 1 minute, and then cover with the stock. Bring to a simmer and cook steadily for 15 minutes, stirring occasionally, until virtually all of the stock has evaporated. Remove the pan from the heat and stir in the peas. Adjust seasoning to taste and spread out on a tray to cool.

2   Heat the vegetable oil in a large, heavy-based saucepan to 180°C | 355F, measuring with a kitchen thermometer for accurate reading.

3   Toss the breadcrumbs, chopped basil and some seasoning in a bowl.

4   Take small handfuls of the left over risotto and enclose around a tablespoon of the cooled meat sauce. Roll the risotto balls in the breadcrumb mixture to coat, arranging them on a lined tray.

5   Once the oil has reached the correct temperature, deep-fry 3–4 balls at a time until golden-brown and crisp, 3–4 minutes.

6   Carefully remove from the oil with a slotted spoon, draining on kitchen paper. Repeat until all the arancini have been deep-fried.

Panzanella

Ingredients:
1 stale crusty loaf, torn into chunks
2 tbsp rice wine vinegar
75 ml | ⅓ cup extra-virgin olive oil
6 large vine tomatoes, cut into
wedges
1 red onion, thinly sliced
2 tbsp basil leaves, torn
salt and freshly ground black pepper

Prep and cook time: 30 minutes
Makes: 4 servings

1   Mix together the vinegar and oil in a large bowl.

2   Add the remaining ingredients and stir well to coat. Cover and leave to sit at room temperature for 20 minutes.

3   Spoon into bowls and serve at room temperature.

'Can I eat the children's food?'

It can seem slightly ridiculous for an adult to want to eat things that have been specially prepared for a child. In a restaurant, we'd probably be too embarrassed to choose something for ourselves from the kids' menu; we have to suppress our curiosity about the smiley face pizza or the soup with animal crackers. But secretly we may be charmed by the soft textures, mild flavours and funny shapes.

Our attraction isn't merely linked to taste: through such foods, we're hovering around distant (but powerful) memories of being little – when we were cared for and looked after; when we had no responsibilities; when we were loved just for existing; when we could be thrilled by a snowfall or a puddle; when people carried us if we got tired, and when we didn't have complicated emotional drives and dark bodily urges.

There's a benign kind of regression activated by certain foods in which we reconnect with what was lovely and good about our early years. We are back in touch with our warm readiness to be loved; our enthusiasm for simple things; our sense of trust and admiration; our hopefulness.

We're not becoming 5 years old again, but thanks to a curly fry or alphabet spaghetti, we're letting the best parts of who we were in childhood enter into dialogue with the more forbidding, complicated and sadder creatures we have become.

Eating off our own children's plates is also confirmation of the deep ties of loyalty and love that connect us to our offspring. When they have run off to play in the garden and we are left at table (too tired as yet to start clearing up), we might reach over and munch on the bit of sausage smeared with tomato sauce they abandoned; we'll eat the remains of their sandwich or finish an apple they've taken three bites from or finish the remainder of a half-eaten fish finger. Such things would be disgusting if we did them in a work canteen or if, on a plane, we stretched over and scooped up the remains of a ham sandwich on the tray of the stranger sitting next to us. But around our children, such picking becomes an act of precious intimacy. We're demonstrating our closeness by eating not just the same kind of food, but the same bits of food, perforated by the slender imprints of their milk teeth.

For the child who comes in and sees us devouring the last of their beans or mousse, it's perhaps lovely to witness their parent wanting what's on their plate so badly. The child can see that they have something the parent really wants, when too often, it is the child who is envious of the parent's possessions: the electric saw they're not allowed to touch; the car they can't possibly drive; the credit card the adult waves in shops. For a moment, in the company of mini-burgers or green peas, the hierarchy is reversed and it's the child's situation that is established as more appealing and profound.

Homemade fish fingers

Ingredients:

1 egg
100 g | 4 oz panko breadcrumbs
1 tbsp light olive oil
400 g | 14 oz skinless and boneless
white fish, such as haddock

Prep time: 10 minutes
Cook time: 20 minutes
Makes: 4 servings

1   Heat oven to 200°C (180° fan) | 400F | gas 6. Beat the egg and pour into a shallow dish. Put the panko breadcrumbs, salt and pepper into a separate shallow dish.

2   Brush a non-stick baking sheet with half the oil. Dip the fish strips into the egg, then roll them in the breadcrumbs. Transfer to the baking sheet and bake for 20 minutes until golden.

3   Serve the fish fingers with peas, chips and plenty of ketchup.

Mini-burgers

Ingredients:

For the buns:

275 g | 2 cup self-raising flour, sifted,
plus extra as needed
1 tsp dried oregano
½ tsp dried rosemary
½ tsp salt
60 g | ¼ cup butter, cubed
250 ml buttermilk

For the mini-burgers:

450 g | 3 cups beef mince, at least
15% fat
1 small onion, diced
1 handful flat-leaf parsley, chopped
1 tsp Dijon mustard
1 tsp Worcestershire sauce
1 tsp salt
½ tsp freshly ground black pepper
4 Cheddar cheese slices, cut in half

To serve:

tomato ketchup

Prep and cook time: 50 minutes
Makes: 8 burgers, 4 servings

1   For the buns: Preheat the oven to 230°C (210° fan) | 450F | gas 8. Grease and line two baking trays with greaseproof paper.

2   Stir together the flour, herbs and salt in a large mixing bowl. Add the butter and rub into the flour mixture until rough breadcrumbs form.

3   Stir in the buttermilk until a rough dough forms. Turn out onto a lightly floured surface and pat down into a round.

4   Roll out to 0.75 cm | ⅓" thickness and cut out at least 16 rounds using a small cookie cutter. Arrange between the lined trays, spaced apart.

5   Bake for 8–10 minutes until risen and golden all over. Remove from the oven and set the trays on wire racks, letting the buns cool on the trays.

6   For the burgers: Preheat the grill to hot. Scrunch together all the ingredients for the burgers, apart from the Cheddar, in a mixing bowl.

7   Divide and shape into eight small, thick patties. Arrange on a grilling tray and grill for 8–10 minutes, turning occasionally, until firm to the touch and well-browned all over.

8   Remove from the grill, top with Cheddar, and return to the grill for a minute or so until the cheese has melted.

9   Remove from the grill and top with some tomato ketchup. Sandwich each patty between two buns and serve.

'Dare I be a bit bad?'

Of course, there are people who should try a lot harder to be good. But for most of us, the problem lies elsewhere: we're already predisposed to making our best efforts; we're dutiful and responsible, ready to abide by the rules and devoted to trying to do the right thing. Indeed, we've grown a little sick from trying so hard to measure up.

Our culture generally isn't good at lessening the strain on an already severe conscience and allowing the less righteous sides of a personality some freedom. At the root of the prevailing moralism is a thesis about the relationship between justice and effort: if we are good, we will be rewarded. If we work hard, our careers will flourish; if we are polite and modest, we'll have nice friends. If we are kind, we will find love. And if we regulate our diets in all the ways experts tell us, we'll be healthy and live a long time.

It's a powerful idea, stemming originally from a religious belief that virtue will be rewarded in the eyes of God. But in reality, life does not reliably live up to this vision of justice. Our efforts don't routinely result in us getting what we want. We put in long hours but the company we work for gets into difficulty because of an ill-judged expansion in Eastern Europe for which we were not responsible – and we are sacked. Or we try hard to listen to our partner, but our sex life withers all the same and we end up getting divorced; or a friend who was careful around what they ate still gets cancer and dies before their 35th birthday.

Our bet on the link between being good and getting our just reward doesn't reliably pay off. It's not surprising, and should indeed be celebrated, that at times we get fed up with self-abnegation and the frustration of our promises. We're not simply weakening: we're making a proper protest against the injustice of reality. We're not going to go off the rails entirely. However, if we're occasionally naughty and strategically 'bad', we're acknowledging a darker fact about existence: effort, sadly, is no guarantee of a good outcome.

The occasional indulgence around food makes a metaphysical statement: the cosmos is not a moral machine. We're accepting a tragic dimension in life: the person who does the right thing can still meet with a grim fate. We should, at points, knowing that the good do die young and the talented and hard-working fail, enjoy the pleasures of 'bad' foods.

Five cheese macaroni

Ingredients:
300 g | 10 oz | 2 ½ cups macaroni
40 g | 2 ½ tbsp butter
40 g | 2 ½ tbsp plain flour
500 ml | 2 cups milk
100g | 3 ½ oz of each of the following
cheeses – you can substitute with
whatever your favourites might be:
gorgonzola, cheddar, Caerphilly
1 tsp wholegrain mustard

½ tsp nutmeg
100 g | 3 ½ oz mozzarella, chopped
50 g | 2 oz freshly grated Parmesan
75 g | 2 ½ oz fresh breadcrumbs

Prep and cook time: 30 minutes
Makes: 4 servings

1   Preheat the grill to high.

2   Cook the macaroni in a large saucepan of salted, boiling water until just tender to the bite (*al dente*), about 10 minutes.

3   While the pasta is cooking make your white sauce. Heat the butter in a separate saucepan until melted, then whisk in the flour until smooth and cook for a couple of minutes. Whisk in the milk gradually, waiting until the mixture has thickened before adding any more. Once all the milk has been incorporated add the gorgonzola, cheddar and Caerphilly to the same pot. Stir until melted. Add the wholegrain mustard and season with nutmeg, salt and pepper.

4   When the pasta has finished cooking, drain and stir into the cheese sauce. Mix well.

5   Transfer into a large ovenproof dish and top generously with the mozzarella, Parmesan and breadcrumbs.

6   Grill for 4–5 minutes or until the top is golden and bubbling.

The Nihilist's ice cream sundae with chocolate sauce

Ingredients:

Chocolate sauce:

40 ml | 2 ½ tbsp double cream

30 g | 1 tbsp golden syrup

20 g | 1 ½ tbsp caster sugar

1 tbsp cocoa powder, sifted

40 g | 1 ½ oz dark chocolate, (min. 70% cocoa), roughly chopped

10 g | 1 tbsp unsalted butter

To assemble:

500 ml ice cream

To decorate:

maraschino cherries

wafer curls

whipped cream

Prep and cook time: 15 minutes

Makes: 4 servings

1   Combine the cream, golden syrup, sugar, cocoa powder and half of the chocolate in a pan over a medium heat. Bring to a simmer, take off the heat and then stir in the remaining chocolate and butter.

2   Spoon a little of the chocolate sauce into a sundae glass. Layer with scoops of vanilla and chocolate ice cream.

3   Top with whipped cream, wafer curls and a maraschino cherry.

Most recipes don't tell you explicitly how to make sure that a pastry crust goes soggy, or how to ensure that a soup that is meant to be clear can be made to turn out cloudy.
But perhaps they should.

'In praise of the dish that
goes wrong'

Instead of being a deep, bright runny
yellow, our scrambled eggs are
pale and flaky; instead of reaching
the plate as a whole, firm slice, the
salmon has broken off into a dozen
messy fragments; the crust of our pie
doesn't rise into a neat glowing dome
but sags anaemically and caves in in
the centre.

We might be tempted to throw it
all away, but we shouldn't. As we
continue with these apparently
woeful but actually tasty meals, we're
signalling an important general truth
to ourselves: something can be wrong
and look and sound a little awful and
still be good enough.

Most recipes don't tell you explicitly
how to make sure that a pastry crust
goes soggy, or how to ensure that a
soup that is meant to be clear can be
made to turn out cloudy. But perhaps
they should.

By embarking on cooking projects
that are likely to turn out badly
(judged by an ideal standard) but
are still good enough to eat, we are
keeping in touch with the truth that
we can fail by the standards of an
overly ambitious world, yet still be fine
and, on some days, truly happy.

Beef wellington

Ingredients:

For the duxelles:

450 g | 1 lb mushrooms, chopped
50 g | 2 oz butter
2 medium shallots, minced
1 sprig fresh thyme, chopped
½ cup dry vermouth or white wine
sea salt

For the beef wellington:

1kg | 2lb 4oz beef fillet of even
thickness
2 tbsp olive oil
1 tbsp English mustard
8–12 slices Parma ham
400 g | 14 oz block puff pastry
1 tbsp flour, for dusting
1 egg, beaten

Cook and prep time: 2 ½ hours
Serves: 6

1   For the duxelles: Prepare the duxelles the day before.

2   Pulse the mushrooms in a food processor until very finely chopped.

3   Heat butter in a pan over a medium heat and add the mushrooms, shallots and thyme. Cook out as much of the moisture as possible. Season.

4   Add the vermouth to the pan and cook for a further 10 minutes or until all the liquid has been absorbed. Remove from the heat and chill in the fridge.

5   For the beef wellington: Trim any sinew from the beef and season well with salt.

6   Heat oil in a cast iron pan over a high heat. Brown the beef fillet on all sides for 8–10 minutes, remove from the pan, brush with mustard and leave to cool completely.

7   Spread a large piece of clingfilm out on to a work surface. Lay the Parma ham on top, overlapping slightly so that it forms a rectangle large enough to cover the beef fillet.

8   Spread the duxelles on top of the ham in an even layer, then place the beef in the middle.

9   Grasping the end of the clingfilm, roll the ham and duxelles around the beef to form a tight cylinder. Twist the ends of the clingfilm to secure and chill for 15 minutes.

10   Dust the work surface lightly with flour. Roll out the puff pastry into a rectangle approximately 10 cm | 4" wider than then shortest side of the beef.

11   Unwrap the beef and place on top of the pastry. Brush the surrounding pastry with some of the beaten egg. Fold the pastry over the short ends then roll the beef in the pastry until it is completely encased, pressing the edges to seal. Trim excess pastry with a sharp knife.

12   Turn the wellington over so that the seam is on the underside. Place on a baking tray and brush all over with the remaining egg. Use a sharp knife to lightly score a decorative pattern in the wellington. Sprinkle with sea salt. Leave to chill for another 30 minutes.

13   Heat oven to 200°C (180° fan) | 400F | gas 6.

14   Place the wellington in the middle of the oven and cook until pastry is golden brown – approximately 30 minutes. Test with a meat thermometer for an accurate result (medium rare: 55°C | 130F). Allow to rest for at least 10 minutes before serving.

6
Food for thinking

Food for Thinking

'Transcendent Thinking'
Lavender, blackberry and pineapple juice 309
Cinnamon nut muesli 310
Garlic, ginger, turmeric broth 311
Beetroot carpaccio with star anise 312

'Nimble Thinking'
Warm quinoa, spinach and shiitake salad 316
Walnut-miso noodles 317
Lean green mint smoothie 318

'Sensuous Thinking'
Gruyère, mustard and pickle sandwiches 321
Tomato and Parmesan tart 322
Scotch eggs 324

'Creative Thinking'
A dish to prepare:
Roasted pigeon with celeriac puree, cavolo nero,
blackcurrant and red-wine sauce 328
Things to eat:
Edamame beans 332

'Virtuous Thinking'
Seaweed salad 336
Lentil stew with kale 337
Tuna sashimi with wasabi sauce 338
Glasses of water, drunk very slowly,
and nothing more between 7am and 7pm.
Unleavened, salt-free matzos crackers,
One apple, cut in slices with a sharp knife. 341

One of the tragedies of the way we are built is that we know intuitively that we could be much cleverer and more insightful than we generally are, if only we knew how to extract the best thoughts from our elusive, cavernous, intermittent minds.

Every so often, at seemingly random moments, a useful thought will emerge, but we don't understand its genesis and it may be too late to use it properly. We may realise a month after an important meeting what we should have said about a deal to our colleagues; in the middle of the night it occurs to us what our upset two mornings ago was really about; in retrospect we might see how we made things difficult for our partner, though by now the relationship is over.

Typically we imagine that good thinking is something that just spontaneously happens (or doesn't). Ideas pop up; words appear; questions form themselves, but we don't usually have a sense that these are processes over which we have much control.

However, there's another side to our experience. We know that many things do alter our mentality: what we eat and drink can markedly affect the kind of thoughts that manifest themselves. At an extreme, alcohol reduces inhibitions and may (for a while) lead to the foregrounding of positive, ambitious notions. Coffee might sharpen our strength for a more demanding cognitive task.

Such examples point to a more general – and often much more subtle – possibility: all foods are, in a sense, drugs. Usually we reserve the term 'drugs' for prohibited substances, but most things we ingest have an effect on our minds and are 'drugs' in the general sense of altering our states of consciousness; it's just that we haven't charted their influence on us in much detail and the law doesn't care about them. Chocolate is, in this sense, a drug, as is Stilton and apple crumble.

We can use food strategically to shift our inner atmosphere. What we eat connects us to different parts of who we are. What follows are descriptions of different modes of thought, and a few of the foods that might most readily promote them.

'Transcendent Thinking'

Normally, our thoughts revolve tightly around our own ego: What do I want? What am I afraid of? What will happen to me next year?

Then, occasionally, something remarkable happens. We go beyond – or 'transcend' – our own tightly circumscribed selves and start to think in more generous, broad ways about humanity and our vulnerable planet. We start to care and identify ourselves with a greater range of peoples, ages and creeds. We perceive that the appropriate response to humanity is not fear, cynicism or aggression, but love. The world reveals itself as quite different: a place of suffering and misguided effort, full of people striving to be heard and lashing out against others, but also a place of tenderness and longing, beauty and touching vulnerability.

Our own lives now feel less precious. We can with tranquillity contemplate being no longer present. The gap between 'me' and 'not-me' is reduced: we imaginatively blend with natural things, of which (we now see) we have always been a part: trees, the wind, a moth, clouds or waves breaking on the shore. From this point of view,

status is nothing, possessions don't matter, grievances lose their urgency. If certain people could encounter us at this point, they might be amazed at our transformation and at our new-found generosity and empathy.

Transcendent states are often desperately short-lived: a few moments late at night or at dusk; on a plane or train journey across wide open country. But we can, through certain ingredients (especially lavender, cardamom, turmeric and cinnamon), access them a little more systematically and thereby loosen the grip of our insistent egos.

Lavender, blackberry and pineapple juice

Ingredients:
300 g | 11 oz | 2 cups blackberries
a few drops lavender essence,
see Tips
750 ml | 26 fl oz | 3 cups
pineapple juice
ice cubes
sparkling water, chilled

Prep time: 10 minutes
Makes: 4 servings

1   Puree the blackberries in a food processor or blender. Pass the puree through a fine sieve into a pitcher and add the lavender essence and pineapple juice, stirring well; add more lavender to taste, as needed.

2   Fill glasses with ice cubes before filling with the juice and topping up with sparkling water.

Tips
Lavender essence is available from good online retailers and some cookware shops; make sure it is baking-grade and safe for consumption.

Cinnamon nut muesli

Ingredients:

120 g | 1 cup almonds
65 g | ½ cup walnuts
65 g | ½ cup pecans
70 g | 1 cup coconut flakes
120 g | ½ cup raw coconut oil
2 tbsp smooth peanut butter
2 tsp ground cinnamon
2 tbsp cocoa powder
3 tbsp sesame seeds

2 tbsp chia seeds
full-fat Greek yoghurt, to serve
(optional)

Prep and cook time: 25 minutes
Makes: 8 servings

1   Preheat the oven to 180°C (160° fan) | 350F | gas 4. Spread out the nuts and coconut flakes on a rimmed baking tray.

2   Bake in the oven until golden and lightly toasted, about 10 minutes. Remove from the oven and let cool briefly before roughly chopping.

3   Melt the coconut oil and peanut butter in a large saucepan set over a medium heat, stirring to combine.

4   Remove from the heat and whisk in the cinnamon and cacao powder. Stir in the toasted nuts and coconut flakes, as well as the sesame seeds and chia seeds.

5   Turn out the muesli onto a rimmed baking tray lined with parchment paper. Let the mixture cool completely before breaking up and storing in an airtight jar.

6   When ready to serve, spoon over bowls of Greek yoghurt if desired.

Garlic, ginger, turmeric broth

Ingredients:
2 heads garlic, split horizontally
1 thumb fresh ginger, thinly sliced
2 fresh bay leaves,
or 3 dried bay leaves
1 tbsp ground turmeric
1 tsp black peppercorns
1 tsp coriander seeds
2 tbsp chilli oil (optional)
1 handful coriander, torn

1 ½ litres vegetable stock
sea salt
freshly ground black pepper

Prep and cook time: 45 minutes
Makes: 4 servings

1   Place the garlic, ginger, bay leaves, turmeric, peppercorns, and coriander seeds in a saucepan. Cover with the stock.

2   Bring to the boil and then reduce to a gentle simmer for 30 minutes.

3   Strain the broth into a clean saucepan and return to a boil over a moderate heat, letting it reduce by about one-quarter.

4   Once reduced, season to taste and stir in the chilli oil, if using.

5   Divide between bowls and garnish with coriander.

Beetroot carpaccio with star anise

Ingredients:
250 ml | 1 cup rice vinegar
1 star anise
4 pods cardamom
1 stick cinnamon
1 tbsp sugar
½ tsp sea salt
250 g | 1 ½ cup cooked beetroot, thinly sliced, see Tips

Dressing:
50ml | 3 tbsp honey
¼ tsp sea salt

1 tbsp dried oregano
1 tsp dried thyme

Garnish:
2 tsp olive oil
2 tbsp soft goat's cheese
Handful of toasted hazelnuts
Fresh mint

Prep and cook time: 1 hour 20 minutes
Makes: 4 servings

1   Combine vinegar, spices, sugar, salt and beetroot in a bowl. Cover and marinade at room temperature for 1 hour.

2   Meanwhile, prepare the dressing by combining honey, salt, and dried herbs in a bowl. Set aside.

3   To serve, drain marinade from beetroot. Spoon one tablespoon of the dressing into the bowl and toss gently to mix. Arrange the beetroot onto a platter, drizzle with remaining dressing and garnish with olive oil, goat's cheese, hazelnuts and mint.

Tips
Slice beetroot with a mandolin for the thinnest carpaccio.

In our new frame of mind, obstacles disappear; we think our way out of conundrums; we bypass dilemmas that had held us up for months.

'Nimble Thinking'

Most of the time, our thinking is ponderous, predictable and slow. We travel repetitively down familiar byways of the mind. We are a little pessimistic, if not a touch depressed. But occasionally, we access a far nimbler, quicker, more impetuous and more imaginative mood. It is as if consciousness had magically grown long legs and could now take huge strides across a mental landscape we'd previously been crawling over. In our new frame of mind, obstacles disappear; we think our way out of conundrums; we bypass dilemmas that had held us up for months.

We can suddenly imagine trying things in a completely new way. We might wholly reorder an aspect of our lives. Perhaps we can transform a relationship through a bold conversation; maybe our work life can go in a new direction through an inspired original venture. The horizon expands; we can make sense not just of the next few days but of the coming years. Our minds feel light and free; it is as if the dust and cobwebs have been cleared away from the windscreen of consciousness and we now see the horizon and the distant landscape more clearly.

Warm quinoa, spinach and shiitake salad

Ingredients:

250 g | 9 oz | 1 ½ cups quinoa, thoroughly rinsed
750 ml | 26 fl oz | 3 cups chicken or vegetable stock
150 g | 5 oz | 6 cups baby spinach, washed
2 tbsp olive oil
250 g | 9 oz | 3 cups shiitake mushrooms, roughly chopped

1 clove garlic, finely chopped
½ lemon, juiced
sea salt
freshly ground black pepper

Prep and cook time: 35 minutes
Makes: 4 servings

1   Place the quinoa in a large saucepan and cook over a medium heat until dried out and starting to toast.

2   Cover with the stock, stir well, and bring to a simmer over a medium heat. Once simmering, cover with a lid and cook over a low heat for 15–20 minutes until tender.

3   Remove the quinoa from the heat. Remove the lid, scatter the spinach on top, and then re-cover and leave to cool to one side.

4   In the meantime, heat the oil in a large frying or sauté pan set over a moderate heat until hot. Add the shiitake mushrooms, garlic and a generous pinch of salt, sautéing until golden, about 5–7 minutes.

5   Fluff the quinoa with a fork to separate the grains and mix in the spinach. Fold in the shiitake mushrooms and season to taste with lemon juice, salt and pepper.

6   Divide between bowls and serve warm for best results.

Walnut-miso noodles

Ingredients:
75 g | 2 ½ oz | ½ cup walnuts
4 tbsp sunflower oil
1 clove garlic, crushed
2 tbsp white miso paste
2 tbsp rice wine vinegar
1 tsp honey
250 g | 9 oz soba noodles
250 g | 9 oz | 2 cups asparagus,
woody ends removed, spears thinly
sliced on bias
1 tbsp sesame seeds
2 spring onions, green tops only,
finely sliced
sea salt

Prep and cook time: 15 minutes
Makes: 4 servings

1   Lightly toast the walnuts in a dry frying pan set over a medium heat until aromatic and golden-brown, about 1–2 minutes.

2   Tip out into a food processor and add the oil, garlic, miso paste, vinegar, honey and a pinch of salt, processing until a dressing forms. Set aside until needed.

3   Cook the noodles in a large saucepan of boiling water until just tender to the bite, about 2–3 minutes; add the asparagus to the water after the noodles have been cooking for 1 minute.

4   Drain well and refresh the noodles and asparagus in a large bowl of iced water. Drain again and spread out on kitchen paper to dry out.

5   When ready to serve, transfer the noodles and asparagus to a mixing bowl. Add the prepared dressing and sesame seeds, tossing to combine.

6   Divide between bowls and garnish with sliced spring onions before serving.

Lean green mint smoothie

Ingredients:

500 ml | 2 cups water
250 g | 1 cup mango, frozen
500 g | 2 cups spinach
500 g | 2 cups kale, coarsely chopped
Handful of mint

Prep and cook time: 2 minutes
Makes: 2 servings

1   Blitz all of the ingredients in a powerful food processor until smooth.
Add more water for the desired consistency.

'Sensuous Thinking'

We typically associate intellectuals with high-quality thinking. However, so-called clever people are prey to a characteristic defect: a tendency to over-abstraction, and a loss of connection with the bodily and the sensuous. Reason can become too dominant for its own good.

We can fall in with a sort of thinking that is technically impressive but emotionally arid and cut off from actual experience. We may fixate on certain ideas that are academically sound but have no power to move or motivate an audience.

Being 'over-intellectual' can mean forgetting or ignoring a raft of things that legitimately matter within the overall economy of a good life. The over-intellectual designer might produce a chair that makes a provocative allusion to mid-20th-century Bauhaus philosophy, but is appallingly uncomfortable to sit on; the over-intellectual political advisor might come up with an idea that is theoretically brilliant but turns into a disaster on the ground because it fails to factor in certain emotional realities of real inhabitants; the over-intellectual historian gets all the facts right but neglects to tell a good story.

The wise countermove isn't to throw away one's intelligence but to add something to it; to strive to integrate it with memory, desire, taste, smell and visceral experience. If we're prone to being excessively intellectual, we need to keep reminding ourselves of the central appeal of non-intellectual things. Food is perhaps the leading way we can reawaken, through our palate, our dormant, threatened connections with the sensory realm.

We should be particularly alive to the potential of eating outdoors. The philosopher Jean-Jacques Rousseau (1712–78), knowing his tendencies to over-intellectual abstraction, took care (in the summer months in Switzerland) to eat at least one meal a day either in a forest or by the side of the lake of Geneva. Anyone with a PhD (or aspirations in this direction) would be advised to pay close attention to the significance of picnics for the regulation of their minds.

Gruyère, mustard and pickle sandwiches

Ingredients:

8 slices of bread
4 tbsp butter, softened
2–4 tbsp Dijon mustard
200 g | 7 oz Gruyère, thinly sliced
2–4 large gherkins, in vinegar, drained
and thinly sliced

Prep and cook time: 5 minutes
Makes: 4 servings

1   Spread four bread slices with butter and the remaining four slices with the mustard; adjust the amount of mustard to suit your tastes.

2   Top the buttered bread slices with Gruyère and gherkin slices. Sit the other bread slices on top, mustard facing down.

3   Wrap in greaseproof paper or a sandwich bag and enjoy by the nearest forest or lake (failing that, a park will do).

Tomato and Parmesan tart

Ingredients:

For the pastry:

300 g | 11 oz | 2 ½ cups plain flour
½ tsp salt
¼ tsp baking powder
150 g | 5 oz | ⅔ cup unsalted butter, cold and cubed
3–4 tbsp iced water
1 large egg, beaten with 1 tbsp water

For the filling:

4 heirloom tomatoes
80 g | 3 oz | ½ cup sun-dried tomatoes, in oil, drained and roughly sliced
4 tbsp olive oil
1 clove garlic, minced
1 tsp dried oregano
½ tsp dried basil
1 handful basil leaves
50 g | 1 ¾ oz Parmesan, for shaving
freshly ground black pepper

Prep and cook time: 1 hour 20 minutes
Makes: 4 servings

1   For the pastry: Combine the flour, salt, baking powder, and butter in a food processor.

2   Pulse until the mixture resembles rough breadcrumbs. Add the iced water, 1 tablespoon at a time, and pulse between additions until a rough dough comes together.

3   Turn out the dough onto a floured surface and knead briefly. Wrap in clingfilm and chill for 30 minutes.

4   After chilling, remove the dough from the fridge and preheat the oven to 180°C (160° fan) | 350F | gas 4.

5   Roll out the dough into a 23 cm | 9" wide round, approximately ½ cm | ¼" thick on a lightly floured surface.

6   Transfer to a 23 cm | 9" tart tin, crimping the edge of the pastry to build a border. Prick all over with a fork and brush with the beaten egg wash.

7   For the filling: Thinly slice the tomatoes on a mandoline set to a fine setting; you can also do this freehand with a sharp chef's knife. Arrange in the pastry along with the sun-dried tomatoes, seasoning with a little salt.

8   Whisk together the olive oil, garlic, and dried herbs in a mixing bowl. Brush over the tomatoes on the pastry.

9   Bake for about 25–30 minutes until the pastry is cooked through and golden underneath.

10 Remove from the oven and and let stand briefly before serving with a garnish of basil leaves, freshly ground black pepper, and a some freshly shaved Parmesan.

Scotch eggs

Ingredients:

8 large eggs

600 g | 21 oz | 4 cups pork sausage

1 tbsp Dijon mustard

1 tsp sage

1 tsp thyme

1 tsp parsley

70 g | 2 ½ oz | ½ cup cornflour

180 g | 6 oz | 2 cups panko breadcrumbs

1.5 l | 53 fl oz | 6 cups vegetable oil, for deep-frying

sea salt

freshly ground black pepper

Prep and cook time: 40 minutes

Makes: 6 servings

1   Carefully lower six of the eggs in a large saucepan of boiling water. Boil for 6 minutes before removing and refreshing in a large bowl of iced water.

2   Drain again and carefully peel. Rinse off any shell and pat dry with kitchen paper.

3   Remove and discard the sausage casing. Combine the pork, mustard, herbs and plenty of salt and pepper in a large mixing bowl. Scrunch together with your hands to combine.

4   Divide the mixture into six even portions and gently shape around the peeled eggs, totally enclosing them with the pork mixture.

5   Place the cornflour in a shallow dish. Beat the remaining eggs with some salt and pepper in a second shallow dish. Place the panko breadcrumbs in a third shallow dish.

6   Dust the shaped eggs with cornflour, shaking off any excess. Dip into the beaten egg to coat and let the excess drip off before rolling in the panko to coat.

7   Arrange on a greaseproof paper-lined baking tray. Cover and chill as you heat the oil.

8   Heat the oil to 180°C | 350F in a heavy-based saucepan, using a thermometer to accurately gauge the temperature.

9   When the oil is ready, deep-fry the Scotch eggs in the hot oil, three at a time, until golden-brown and crisp, about 4 minutes.

10 Using a slotted spoon, remove to a tray lined with kitchen paper to drain. Cover loosely with aluminium foil to keep warm as you deep-fry the remaining Scotch eggs.

'Creative Thinking'

We might suppose that the best place to think creatively would be a large room with a big desk, complete quiet, plenty of natural light and a window with a view – perhaps onto water or a park. But this assumption is not really true to the way our minds work. The primary obstacle to thinking up new, useful and original ideas is not a cramped desk or an uninteresting horizon; it is, first and foremost, anxiety. The most profound thoughts we need to grapple with typically have a slightly disturbing character. If we were to pinpoint them accurately and get clear about their significance, there could be a risk. We might discover that some of our past cherished beliefs were not as wise as we'd supposed; we might realise that we were previously wrong about something; we might have to make some significant and tricky changes to our lives.

As these potential implications start to come into view, our inner censor, motivated by a desire for calm rather than growth, becomes alarmed. The potential for creativity shuts down. A vigilant part of the self gets agitated; it distracts us, it makes us feel tired or gives us a strong need to go online. Skilfully, it confuses and muddles our train of thought. It blocks the progress we were starting to make towards creative concepts that – though important and interesting – also presented marked threats to short-term peace.

That is why one of the best ways to think creatively is to give ourselves something other to do besides simply thinking. Going for a walk in the woods works well: we're so taken up with putting one foot in front of the other, the more original ideas that have been half-forming at the back of our minds have a chance to reach consciousness. We're not meant to be thinking, so we can think freely and courageously. Without knowing quite how it happens, brilliant ideas pop into our heads as we navigate around the roots of ancient mossy trees.

This quality of sufficient but not overwhelming distraction might also be present when we're driving down the highway or swimming in a lake; when there's just enough for the managerial timid side of the mind to be doing to keep it from interfering with our more authentic and bolder inner machinations.

Food can help with this kind of creative thinking in two distinct ways. First, when we're preparing a complicated dish, most of our powers of thought will be taken up with following a recipe, but there will be just enough room left for wilder, more speculative ideas to break through. We might find that a sequence of precious ideas come to us as we're watching a sauce thicken or basting the underside of a pigeon.

Second, in terms of eating, there are snacks and lighter dishes that play a role similar to a walk or a swim: they distract our minds just enough to allow them to release their trapped insights. We can sit with a bowl in a comfortable chair and, while ostensibly peeling beans or cracking open pistachios or walnuts, be subtly working on extracting precious content from our minds.

The American essayist Ralph Waldo Emerson (1803–82) once wrote: 'In the minds of geniuses, we find our own neglected thoughts.' In other words, so-called geniuses don't have thoughts different from the ones most of us have; they're just better at not allowing their inhibitions and preconceptions to get in the way of entertaining them. They've found ways to access the thoughts we all have, but are generally too anxious and procedural to pay attention to.

We should get a lot more imaginative about what real thinking is and where it happens. We should learn that the real enemy of creative thinking isn't a small desk or a modest view: it is almost always anxiety, for which there can be few better cures than a bowl of edamame beans or the task of working up a complex pigeon dish.

A dish to prepare:
Roasted pigeon with celeriac puree, cavolo nero, blackcurrant and red-wine sauce

Ingredients:
4 whole pigeons
1 onion, finely diced
1 carrot, finely diced
1 celery, finely diced
60 g | ¼ cup butter
1 tbsp honey
250 ml | 1 cup red wine
500 ml | 2 cup chicken stock
Handful of blackberries
1 tbsp olive oil

Celeriac puree :
1 celeriac (approx. 500 g | 1 lb), peeled and cut into small pieces
30 g | 2 tbsp butter
250 ml | 1 cup whole milk
1 pinch sea salt

Cavolo nero:
4–5 leaves of cavolo nero
15 g | 1 tbsp butter

Prep time: 1 hour
Cook time: 1 ½ hours
Makes: 4 servings

1   Preheat the oven to 200°C (180° fan) | 400F | gas 6.

2   Remove the legs from the pigeons and set the crowns to one side. Season the legs with a little salt and pepper and roast in the oven for 10 minutes until golden brown.

3   Meanwhile, melt the butter over a medium heat and then gently sweat the diced onion, celery and carrot for 5 minutes until onion is translucent and soft. Add the honey and allow to caramelise before adding the red wine. Cook down until the liquid has reduced by half.

4   Add the stock and the roasted legs to the sauce and simmer over a low heat for an hour. Strain through a sieve into a clean pan. Stir a handful of blackberries through and cook for a few minutes until the fruit is slightly soft. Set the sauce to one side.

5   Peel the celeriac and dice. Place in a pan, cover with milk and add a knob of butter, bring to the boil and simmer until tender. Blend with a liquidiser until smooth. If dry use a little of the cooking liquid to get the right consistency. Season to taste.

6   Turn the oven up to 240°C (220° fan) | 475F | gas 9.

7   Heat the oil in a pan. When hot, brown the crowns skin side down then place in the oven for 5–6 minutes, the skin should be crisp. Allow to rest for another five minutes, then carve off the breasts.

8   While the meat is resting, blanch a few leaves of cavolo nero in a pan of boiling water and then quickly toss in a pan of foaming butter. Season generously.

9   Arrange the duck and cavolo nero on to plates. Dot the celeriac and sauce around the them. Finish with a few extra fresh blackberries.

One of the best ways to think creatively is to give ourselves something other to do besides simply thinking.

Things to eat:
Edamame beans

Ingredients:

300 g | 2 cups unshelled edamame
1 litre water
3 tbsp sea salt
sesame seeds (optional)

Prep time: 2 minutes
Cook time: 5 minutes
Makes: 4 servings

1   Rub the edamame with 1 tablespoon of the salt to remove the fuzzy hairs on the outside.

2   Bring the water to boil in a large saucepan and add the remaining salt.

3   Add the edamame and cook for between 3-5 minutes.

4   Drain and rinse with cold water to cool. Season with a little more sea salt and sesame seeds if using. Eat by placing the pod into your mouth and sliding the edamame beans out with your teeth. Discard the pod.

At points, we recognise that we are slipping dangerously towards decadence and what we might, for want of a better word, call sinfulness. We're spending too much time on the computer; we're not doing enough work; we aren't devoting time to the people we love; we are selfish and mean-minded; we rarely give back to others. We're on the point of being disgusted with ourselves. We want to become someone different, better and cleaner (inside and out).

Religions have paid great attention to these moods and given them structure and direction. Not coincidentally, they have typically linked up these aspirations for a more virtuous life with a specific diet, involving either little or no food. Judaism prescribes fasting at Yom Kippur; Islam requires that the faithful abstain from eating during daylight hours during Ramadan; Christianity recommends a severely restricted diet in the forty days between Ash Wednesday and Holy Saturday; many Hindus fast for one day each week.

Religions aren't against food. Fasting is a tribute to how much we love eating and how much it dominates our thoughts. But by deliberately depriving ourselves of food, other interests and concerns have a chance to surface: our sorrow for the wrongs we have done others; our devotion to noble ideals; our wish to tone down our bodily lusts and interests.

Even outside of religions, periods of fasting or modest meals are useful to counter a feeling of being out of control. Through our restraint, we're reasserting – in a particularly vivid and basic way – the superiority of the mind over the body; we're practising regaining control over our runaway selves.

The desire to improve ourselves is one of the most powerful we have. We're so often struck by the painful gap between how we are and how we'd like to be. We do and say things we regret; we're not nice to certain people; we have habits we wish we could shed; we long to be more focused, or better at channelling our efforts, or more decisive, or more confident.

Food can function as the vital goad to help us live up to our aspirations for ourselves. Our desire for virtue can become connected to a resolution to eat only the occasional half grapefruit or a green salad as a treat. Small plates of sashimi promise the development of a new, more principled and righteous soul. In certain moods, resistance to French fries isn't just practical, it turns into a moral refusal. We are set on becoming better people, and what is, or is not, on our plates testifies to our ethical ambitions.

Seaweed salad

Ingredients:
2 tbsp rice wine vinegar
1 tbsp almond butter
110 ml avocado oil
300 g | 2 cups firm tofu, cubed
55 g | ⅓ cup black sesame seeds
55 g | ⅓ cup white sesame seeds
110 g | 2 cups pink laver seaweed,
roughly chopped
150 g | 3 cups wakame seaweed,
roughly chopped
salt and pepper

Prep and cook time: 15 minutes
Makes: 4 servings

1   Whisk together the rice wine vinegar, almond butter, and seasoning in a small mixing bowl. Whisk in the oil in a slow, steady stream until the dressing has emulsified.

2   Roll the cubes of tofu in the sesame seeds, pressing them gently into the seeds to adhere.

3   Toss the two seaweeds with the dressing and arrange with the tofu cubes in bowls.

Lentil stew with kale

Ingredients:

2 tbsp olive oil
1 onion, finely chopped
2 medium carrots, peeled and diced
2 celery stalks, diced
2 cloves garlic, finely chopped
200 g | 7 oz | 1 cup brown lentils, rinsed
1250 ml | 44 fl oz | 5 cups vegetable stock
150 g | 5 oz | 2 cups curly kale, thick stems removed, leaves roughly chopped
1 pinch red chilli flakes (optional)
Worcestershire sauce
salt
freshly ground black pepper

Prep and cook time: 55 minutes
Makes: 4 servings

1   Heat the oil in a large saucepan set over a medium heat until hot. Add the onion, carrot, celery, garlic, and a pinch of salt, sweating until softened, about 8–10 minutes.

2   Add the lentils, stir well, and cover with the stock. Bring the liquid to the boil, skim away any scum with a ladle, and then simmer steadily until the lentils are tender, about 30 minutes.

3   Stir in the kale and chilli flakes, if using. Return to a simmer and cook until the kale is wilted, about 3–4 minutes. Season to taste with plenty of salt and pepper and a dash of Worcestershire sauce.

4   Divide between bowls and serve with crusty bread on the side.

Tuna sashimi with wasabi sauce

Ingredients:
250 g | 9 oz fresh tuna fillet, see Tips
2 large egg yolks
1 ½ tbsp wasabi paste
2 tbsp rice wine vinegar
salt
150 g | 5 oz | ⅔ cup unsalted butter,
melted and cooled
1 tbsp sesame seeds
2 tbsp pickled ginger

Prep and cook time: 25 minutes
Makes: 4 servings

1   Wrap the tuna fillet in clingfilm and place in the freezer for at least 15 minutes as you prepare the wasabi sauce.

2   Combine the egg yolks, wasabi paste, vinegar, and a pinch of salt in a food processor. Cover and pulse until smooth.

3   With the motor running, slowly drizzle in the melted, cooled butter until a thick emulsion forms; scrape down the sides from time to time, as needed. Season to taste with more salt as needed.

4   Remove the tuna from the freezer and unwrap before thinly slicing with a sharp chef's knife.

5   Pour the wasabi sauce into a small serving bowl and place in the centre of a serving plate or platter.

6   Arrange the tuna around the sauce and sprinkle the sesame seeds on top. Serve with the pickled ginger on the side.

Tips
Use the highest-grade tuna you can find for this recipe as it is crucial to the overall quality of the dish.

Food can function
as the vital goad to help
us live up to our aspirations
for ourselves.

Glasses of water, drunk very slowly,
and nothing more between 7am and 7pm.
Unleavened, salt-free matzos crackers,
One apple, cut in slices with a sharp knife.

Ingredients:
See above

Prep and cook time: 1 minute
Makes: 1 serving

1   Use the time that you would normally spend preparing and eating a meal to contemplate some of the issues that may be troubling you.

2   Instead of clearing the table and washing up pots and pans consider how you might mentally prepare for tomorrow.

III

Convers-ation

i. Good speaking, good listening

There is broad agreement that every great meal should be accompanied by an equally great conversation. Talking over food is one of the central pleasures of civilisation.

However, our collective assessment of what is required to ensure a good meal on the one hand and a good conversation on the other could not be more different. In the case of the meal, we are ready to make an effort: we buy books, enrol in classes, equip our kitchens with superlative technology, practise our craft and take our time. When it comes to conversation, however, we leave it predominantly to chance. We assume that we'll no more need to plot to have a good conversation than we'd need to plot to have a good sneeze or blink of an eye. We assume that satisfactory discussions are things that happen automatically and cannot be controlled or directed.

As a result of this misplaced Romantic faith, often, over the most succulent and inventive dishes, in the company of profound and kind people, we find ourselves mired in the most banal, emotionally deadening and forgettable exchanges. The talk is fragmented, the guests go off on tangents, we get trapped in superficial dead ends, we swap random anecdotes. By dessert, most of us are so exhausted, we allow one vehement person to hog the stage with their *idée fixe*... We end up leaving the meal certain at once that the fish was perfect and the sorbet unforgettable and that the level of human connection utterly failed to keep up.

The good news is that learning the art of conversation is no more difficult or impossible than learning the art of cookery. We simply need to wake up to the need to do so and take a few steps towards becoming better speakers and better listeners. Improved chat begins with a newfound modesty around our current and historic capacities.

We're liable to be boring at the moment. No one may have told us this directly; our parents love us too much, our friends don't care enough, and our exes couldn't be bothered. But the grim truth is that we have probably been boring our way through most social experiences since the beginning of adulthood.

This is not because we have boring lives; it is because we have the wrong techniques for narrating these lives. Here is some of what goes wrong when we speak:

a) We keep latching onto factual details: we go on about times, places, external movements, not realising that things become interesting only when people say what they feel about what happened, not merely what happened.

b) We often get overwhelmed by an emotion we experienced and insist upon it rather than attempting to explain it. So we say, again and again, 'it was so beautiful' or 'it was the scariest thing in the world' but without accurately unpacking the feeling and thereby being able to make it live in someone else's mind.

c) Just when we promise to get a bit interesting with our narration, we take fright. We get scared of our own emotions, which can threaten to trigger feelings of unbearable sadness, confusion and excitement. We take flight into superficiality.

d) We don't stick with one story. There is so much in our minds, we keep opening up new subplots. As a result, nothing is every properly developed or given a chance to take shape in another's imagination.

The good news is that no one is ever truly boring. We are only in danger of coming across as such when we don't dare (or know how) to communicate our deeper selves to others. The human animal witnessed in its essence, with honesty and without artifice, with all its longings, crazed desires and despair, is always gripping. When we dismiss a person as boring, we are merely pointing to someone who has not had the courage or concentration to tell us what it is like to be them. We invariably prove compelling when we succeed in detailing some of what we crave, envy, regret, mourn and dream.

The interesting person isn't someone to whom obviously and outwardly interesting things have happened: someone who has travelled the world, met important dignitaries or been present at critical geopolitical events. Nor is it someone who speaks in learned terms about the great themes of culture, history or science. They are someone who has grown into an attentive, self-aware listener and a reliable correspondent of their own mind and heart, and who can thereby give us faithful accounts of the pathos, drama and strangeness of being them.

The gift of being interesting is neither exclusive nor reliant on exceptional talent; it requires only honesty and focus. The person we call interesting is in essence someone alive to what we all want from social interaction: an uncensored glimpse of what the brief waking dream called life looks like through the eyes of another person and reassurance that we are not alone with all that feels most bewildering, peculiar and frightening in us.

There is a particular way of discussing oneself that, however long it goes on for, never fails to win friends, reassure audiences, comfort couples, bring solace to the single and buy the good will of enemies: the confession of vulnerability.

To hear that we have failed, that we are sad, that it was our fault, that our partners don't seem to like us much, that we are lonely, that we have wished it might all be over – there is scarcely anything nicer anyone could learn. This is often taken to signal a basic nastiness in human nature, but the truth is more poignant. We are not so much crowing when we hear of failure as reassured to know that we aren't alone with the appalling difficulties of being alive. It is all too easy to suspect that we have been uniquely cursed in the extent of our troubles, of which we seldom find evidence in the lives around us.

We put in so much effort to be perfect. But the irony is that it is failure that charms, because others need to hear external evidence of problems with which we are all too lonely: how un-normal our sex lives are; how arduous our careers are proving; how unsatisfactory our family can be; how worried we are pretty much all the time.

Revealing any of these wounds might place us in danger. Others could laugh; the media could have a field day. That's the point. We get close by revealing things that would, in the wrong hands, be capable of inflicting humiliation on us. Friendship is the dividend of gratitude that flows from an acknowledgement that one has offered something valuable to someone by talking: the key to one's self-esteem and dignity. It's poignant that we should expend so much effort on trying to look strong before the world when it's really the revelation of the somewhat embarrassing, sad, melancholy and anxious bits of us that renders us endearing to others, and transforms strangers into friends.

A good conversation doesn't just require a vulnerable, honest speaker. It also requires a good listener. Being a good listener is one of the most important and enchanting life skills anyone can have. Yet, few of us know how to do it – not because we are evil, but because no one has taught us how, and – a related point – few have listened sufficiently well to us. We come to social life greedy to speak rather than listen, hungry to meet others, but reluctant to hear them. Friendship degenerates into a socialised egoism.

Like most things, the answer lies in education. Our civilisation is full of great books on how to speak – Cicero's *Orator* and Aristotle's *Rhetoric* were two of the greatest in the ancient world – but sadly there is no equivalent significant work called *The Listener*. There is a range of things that the good listener does that makes it so nice to spend time in their company. Without necessarily realising it, we're often propelled into conversation by something that feels both urgent and somehow undefined. We're bothered at work; we're toying with more ambitious career moves; we're not sure if so and so is right for us; a relationship is in difficulties; we're fretting about something or feeling low about life in general; or perhaps we're excited and enthusiastic about something, though the reasons for our passion are tricky to pin down.

At heart, all these are issues in search of elucidation. The good listener knows that, via conversation with another person, we'd ideally move from a confused, agitated state of mind to one that was more focused and (hopefully) more serene. Together with them, we'd work out what was really at stake. In reality, this tends not to happen because there isn't enough of an awareness of the desire and need for clarification within conversation. There aren't enough good listeners. People tend to assert rather than analyse. They restate in many different ways the fact that they are worried, excited, sad or hopeful, and their interlocutor listens but doesn't assist them to discover more.

Good listeners fight against this with a range of conversational gambits. They hover as the other speaks; they offer encouraging remarks of support; they make gentle positive gestures – a sigh of sympathy, a nod of encouragement, a strategic 'hmm' of interest. All the time, they egg the other to go deeper into issues. They love saying: 'tell me more about …'; 'I was fascinated when you said…'; 'why did that happen, do you think?' or 'how did you feel about that?'

The good listener takes it for granted that they will encounter vagueness in the conversation of others. But they don't condemn, rush or get impatient, because they see vagueness as a universal and significant trouble of the mind that it is the task of a true friend to help with. The good listener never forgets how hard, and how important, it is to know our own minds. Often, we're in the vicinity of something, but we can't close in on what's really bothering or exciting us. The good listener knows we benefit from encouragement to elaborate, to go into greater detail, to push a little further.

We need someone who, rather than launching forth, will simply say two magic words: 'Go on….' You mention a sibling and they want to know more. What was the relationship like in childhood? How has it changed over time? They're curious where our concerns and excitements come from. They ask thing like: why did that particularly bother you? Why was that such a big thing for you?

They keep our histories in mind; they might refer back to something we said before and we feel they're building up a deeper base of engagement. It's easy to say vague things: we simply mention that something is lovely or terrible, nice or annoying. But we don't explore why we feel this way. The good listener has a productive, friendly suspicion of some of our own first statements and is after the deeper attitudes lurking in the background. They take things we say like, 'I'm fed up with my job' or 'My partner and I are having a lot of rows...' and help us to concentrate on what it really is about the job we don't like or what the rows might be about deep down. They're bringing to listening an ambition to clear up underlying issues.

A key move of the good listener is not always to follow every byway or sub-plot that the speaker introduces, for they may be getting lost and further from their own point than they would themselves wish. The good listener is helpfully suspicious, knowing that their purpose is to focus the fundamental themes of the speaker rather than veering off with them into every side road. They are always looking to take the speaker back to their last reasonable point, saying, 'Yes, yes, but you were saying just a moment ago...' Or, 'So, what do you think it was about...'

The good listener (paradoxically) is a skilled interrupter. But they don't (as most people do) interrupt to intrude their own ideas; they interrupt to help the other get back to their original more sincere, yet elusive concerns.

The good listener doesn't moralise. They know their own minds well enough not to be surprised or frightened by strangeness. They know how insane we all are; that's why others can feel comfortable being heard by them. They give the impression that they recognise and accept our follies; they don't flinch when we mention a particular desire. They reassure us they're not going to shred our dignity. A big worry in a competitive world is that we feel we can't afford to be honest about how distressed or obsessed we are. Saying one feels like a failure or a pervert could mean being dropped. The good listener signals early and clearly that they don't see us in these terms. Our vulnerability is something they warm to rather than are appalled by.

It is easy to experience ourselves as cursed and deviant or uniquely incapable. But the good listener makes their own strategic confessions so as to set the record straight about the meaning of being a normal (that is, muddled and imperfect) human being. They confess not so much to unburden themselves as to help others accept their own nature and see that being a bad parent, a poor lover or a confused worker are not malignant acts of wickedness, but ordinary features of being alive that others have unfairly edited out of their public profiles.

When we're in the company of people who listen well, we experience a powerful pleasure, but too often we don't realise what this person is doing that is so nice. By paying attention to our feelings of satisfaction, we can learn to magnify them and offer them to others, who will notice, heal and repay the favour in turn. Listening deserves discovery as one of the keys to good meals, and good societies more broadly.

ii. Conversation Menus

In theory, we know that the quality of the questions we ask other people is key to the kinds of conversations we can end up having. But we don't normally think in advance about what questions it might be constructive to ask. Normally we wait for a question to pop into our heads or we fall back on polite but not very inspired staples: Have you got anything special planned for the weekend? What do you do? How are your studies going?

This spur-of-the-moment attitude towards questions is at odds with our general stance around food: typically we go in for planning and preparation. We make lists of things we need to get from the shops; we keep things in the fridge and the cupboard with an eye to meals we'll be making tomorrow or at the weekend.

The ultimate symbol of advanced food planning is the menu. A chef carefully ponders what others might like to eat, gives diners a few options and might vary dishes depending on the season or to fit the needs of a special event.

We have for too long thought of menus in an overly restrictive way, but we can extend the idea of the menu into the realm of conversation. For our meals going forward, we need to operate with both a food and a conversational menu.

What we term a 'Conversation Menu' is a set of questions that covers the three courses we're likely to have.

We can imagine them beautifully designed, placed on the table, an artful invitation to greater ambitions around what is asked and answered. The menus would contain questions that would raise smiles, build friendships and foster the best kind of intimacy, ensuring that the conversation lived up to the food that had occasioned it.

Conversation Menu:
Ambition

FIRST COURSE

Were your parents fulfilled in their ambitions
for themselves?

What were your parents' ambitions for you?

What remains for you to achieve?

Who would you like to impress?

MAIN COURSE

What achievements of others make you jealous?

What personal vulnerabilities and flaws have
held you back in your ambitions?

What, for you, is the relationship between lovability
and achievement?

What is failure for you?

DESSERT

What alternative careers do you suspect you
might be good at?

What price have you paid for your ambitions?

What is the best way to cope with the disapproval
or neglect of the world?

Knowing what you now know, how would you advise
a young person about their ambitions?

Conversation Menu:
Love

FIRST COURSE

Finish this sentence: If someone likes me a lot,
I start to feel…

In what ways are people you are attracted to similar
to one or other of your parents?

On a date, what would you most want to be liked for?

What kinds of suffering would you want a prospective
partner to have experienced in the past?

MAIN COURSE

In what way is your partner (or an ex) annoying?

List five ways in which you are difficult to live with.

In what ways are you not a great communicator?

What's tricky about sex?

DESSERT

Are you good at breaking up?

Which of your ex-partners hurt you the most?

Make a case for why adultery could,
sometimes, be excused.

For which of your flaws would you like to be
treated more generously?

Conversation Menu:
Self-knowledge

FIRST COURSE

How much do you like yourself? What do
you attribute this to?

In what ways are you neurotic (given that we all are)?

What difficulties did your childhood bequeath you?

How might people describe you when you are
not in the room?

MAIN COURSE

What do you find it difficult to communicate directly?

In what contexts do you find it hard to trust people?

What do you characteristically do when you
are emotionally hurt?

In what areas of life would you describe yourself
as immature?

DESSERT

How did your mother leave you feeling about
yourself? And your father?

How do you typically respond to frustration?

What do you think explains why you personally are
more of an introvert or an extrovert? How would
you still like to grow emotionally?

Conversation Menu:
The meaning of life

FIRST COURSE

What problem would you like to solve for others?

Name two meaningful moments you have had.

What is a meaningful conversation in your eyes?

How has your quest for a meaningful life made
relationships and your career more meaningful but
more difficult for you?

MAIN COURSE

Imagine you have five years left to live.
What would you have the confidence to do that you
might previously have lacked?

In my relationships, I would have the confidence to…

In my friendships, I would have the confidence to…

In my work, I would have the confidence to…

With my family, I would have the confidence to...

DESSERT

What's the greatest unhappiness in your
personal life at the moment?

What transcendent experiences have you had?
Where were you? What did they feel like?

What sort of group could you imagine belonging to?
What would it need to be like for you to feel
proud to belong to it?

What advice would you give to your 19-year-old self?
How have you grown since then?

Conversation Menu:
Secrets

FIRST COURSE

Tell your dinner companion a big secret
about yourself.

How do you secretly hope a friend would
describe you at your funeral?

What's the worst thing you've ever done?
Name the general area if the specifics are too tricky.

What negative character flaws do you fear –
in your worst nightmares – that other people have
spotted about you?

MAIN COURSE

List three things about a person close to you that secretly
annoy you (like humming, doing the wrong thing in the
bathroom, being late…)

What sort of things have made you envious recently?

List three (now guilt-inducing) occasions when you
were especially mean to certain people.

What things would alarm your family if they knew?

DESSERT

What are some of your most pervasive insecurities?

What do you worry about in the early hours?

What do you think is quite odd about you?

For which of your flaws would you want to
be forgiven?

Acknowledgments

Photographer:
Tristan Townley

Food stylist:
Seiko Hatfield

Prop stylist:
Claire Piper

Fabrics:
Fermoie (p. 185, 297)

Permissions

10 t   M.Sobreira / Alamy Stock Photo

10 b   Creative Touch Imaging Ltd. / Alamy Stock Photo

11   CC BY 3.0 / Jörg Bittner Unna

12   imageBROKER / Alamy Stock Photo

14 l   Christen Købke, *View of Østerbro from Dosseringen*, 1838. Kunst Museum Winterthur

14 r   Jersey mini dress, Mary Quant, about 1967, England. Museum no. T.86-1982. © Victoria and Albert Museum, London

15   Artokoloro Quint Lox Limited / Alamy Stock Photo

21   Yōshū Chikanobu

108   Jean-Baptiste-Siméon Chardin, *Meal for a Convalescent*, c. 1747. National Gallery of Art, Washington D.C.

145   Jean-Baptiste-Siméon Chardin, *Woman Taking Tea*, 1735. Hunterian Museum and Art Gallery, Glasgow

148   Sandro Botticelli, *The Mystic Nativity*, 1500–1 National Gallery, London

173   Thomas Jones, *A Wall in Naples*, 1782 National Gallery, London

278   DWD-photo / Alamy Stock Photo

281   T.M.O.Buildings / Alamy Stock Photo

282   Jim Laws / Alamy Stock Photo

Index

The School of Life is a global organisation helping people lead more fulfilled lives. It is a resource for helping us understand ourselves, for improving our relationships, our careers and our social lives – as well as for helping us find calm and get more out of our leisure hours. We do this through films, workshops, books, gifts and community. You can find us online, in stores and in welcoming spaces around the globe.